DORSET

A COUNTY HISTORY

Peter Speed

COUNTRYSIDE BOOKS
NEWBURY, BERKSHIRE

First Published 1994
© Peter Speed 1994

COUNTRYSIDE BOOKS
3 Catherine Road
Newbury, Berkshire

ISBN 185306 284 7

The engraving on the title page is dated 1833 and shows
ships off Poole Quay. (Poole Museum Service)

The cover photograph by Roger Holman, shows the view
towards Godmanstone, near Cerne Abbas.

Text illustrated with photographs by the author.
Designed by Mon Mohan.
Produced through MRM Associates Ltd., Reading.
Typeset by The Midlands Book Typesetting Company, Loughborough.
Printed by J.W. Arrowsmith Ltd., Bristol.

Contents

INTRODUCTION

Readers should approach the history of Dorset with an open mind. Many will have gained a notion of the county's past from the grim story of the Tolpuddle Martyrs, as told by the chroniclers of the trade union movement, and from the often grimmer novels of Thomas Hardy. The impression gained from such sources is of a rural backwater inhabited by downtrodden peasants, struggling against oppressive landowners and remorseless Fate. To quite an extent this impression is false.

In the first place, there is no firm historical evidence to suggest that the people of Hardy's Wessex were any worse off than, for example, those of North Oxfordshire, described with such cheerful good humour by Flora Thompson in her delightful *Lark Rise to Candleford*. Hardy is an excellent source on matters of detail, but anyone who wishes to take an objective view of Dorset must first escape from under his sometimes oppressive pall of gloom and doom.

As for being a rural backwater, it is true that Dorset until recently was mainly an agricultural county. But agriculture and its allied trades occupied nine tenths of the people of England until the 18th century, at least half of them as late as 1850, and farming is still one of our most important industries. Moreover, the evidence from Domesday Book onwards suggests that Dorset's farmers were among the best and it is certain that they are, today, some of the most progressive in Europe. This is a marvellous success story, and the saga of the Tolpuddle Martyrs was but a sad consequence of an unhappy period generally for British agriculture.

A book of this length can be only an introduction to Dorset's rich and varied history. Those who wish to investigate further will find plenty of excellent publications, for example those dealing with towns and villages and on individual topics, such as the railways. However, by far the best source is Dorset itself. The landscapes and buildings of the county tell its story far more vividly than any author could ever do. I hope my photographs will help to emphasise this point.

It is my pleasant duty to thank the people who have given me so much invaluable assistance. They include the publishers, the staffs of the Poole, Bournemouth and Canford Cliffs libraries, and the Dorset County Museum. My chief debt is, of course, to my wife, for reasons which are too many to enumerate.

1

THE LAND AND ITS EARLY INHABITANTS

In his admirable *History and Antiquities of the County of Dorset*, 1774, the Rev. John Hutchins said that Dorset consists of three natural regions, the down, the vale and the heath. This division is still helpful in understanding much of the history of the county.

The down is rolling, windswept chalk hills, many of them covered only with a thin soil, full of flints. The grasses are short and fine, so the traditional farming is sheep rearing. Since the chalk has no surface water, the settlements are in the deep, narrow valleys that have been carved by rivers and streams. As well as water, the valleys contain fertile loams.

The vale is undulating country, dissected by streams and with a complicated geology. There are areas, for example around Sherborne and Bridport, where fertile loams overlie limestones and sandstones. Elsewhere, there are sticky clays which defied cultivation for centuries, especially as they were covered with dense forests of broad leaved trees. Generally speaking, the vale produces coarse, rich grass, which is good for cattle.

Most of the heath is too barren to repay cultivation, and was used only for collecting fuel and for rough grazing. There are some comparatively fertile patches, however, around the edges and beside the rivers and streams. These have been farmed, though the settlements were small and widely scattered.

The Isles of Purbeck and Portland do not quite fit into Hutchins's scheme. The north of Purbeck is heathland, next comes a chalk ridge and then a clay vale. Finally, there is a limestone ridge which skirts the sea, so that its southern edge is cliffs. Portland, further south still, is all that remains of another limestone ridge.

Early man evolved some 1.5 million years ago, developing into modern man, or homo sapiens, within the last 300,000 years. These, the first people, belonged to the Palaeolithic or Old Stone Age. They were hunter gatherers who made flint tools, many of which have been found in Dorset's river gravels.

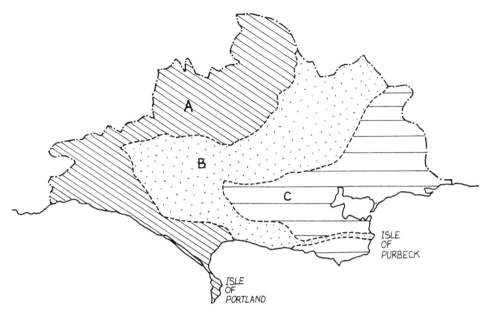

Natural regions of Dorset (A) The vale. Jurassic rocks from 195 ma (million years ago) to 135 ma. Clays in some areas; loams overlaying sandstones and limestones in others. (B) The down. Cretaceous rocks, mainly chalk, from 135 ma to 65 ma. Often, thin stony soils, well drained. (C) The heath. Tertiary deposits since 65 ma. Mainly infertile sands.

The Mesolithic or Middle Stone Age may have begun in about 8000 BC, though this date, like most connected with pre-history, is highly tentative. Again, the people were hunter gatherers, but they did make temporary settlements. Several of these have been excavated in Dorset, one of the most rewarding digs being at Blashenwell, in the Isle of Purbeck. Bones of wild animals such as deer, cattle and pigs were found, along with multitudes of shells from limpets, periwinkles, mussels and cockles.

The first steps towards civilised life based on agriculture were made in the Neolithic or New Stone Age, which began in Britain perhaps in about 4,000 BC. As the people were farmers, they stayed in the same places for years at a time, so they were able to improve old skills, such as tool making, and discover new ones, such as pottery and building.

The folk of the New Stone Age have left some remarkable monuments, the most common being their burial mounds, known as long barrows. These are well named. The one at Pimperne is 350 feet long, 90 feet wide and eight feet high. At Portesham there are some stones known as the 'Grey Mare and her Colts'. Once, they formed the burial chamber and forecourt of a long barrow whose mound has been eroded. A long

Grey Mare and her Colts.

barrow is usually wedge shaped in plan, but there are some burial mounds with parallel sides, called bank barrows. There is one at Long Bredy which is 645 feet long. Long barrows were used for several burials, some at intervals of centuries.

New Stone Age people made causewayed camps. Such a camp is an area surrounded by a bank and a ditch, but it can hardly have been defensive, since the ditch is not continuous. The undisturbed sections form the causeways. There is a causewayed camp on Hambledon Hill, where pottery, and flint and bone tools were discovered.

The henge is yet another type of New Stone Age monument. Again, it is an area surrounded by a bank and a ditch, with the ditch inside the bank. The most impressive henge in Dorset is Maumbury Rings at Dorchester but it is much changed, because the Romans turned it into an amphitheatre and the Roundheads built a gun emplacement on it. At Knowlton there are three henges, the middle one of which is in good condition. It is 350 feet across, is slightly oval in plan and has two entrances. A ruined church stands in the centre, symbolising Christianity's defiance of paganism.

The Dorset Cursus, also from the New Stone Age, is the best example of its kind in England. Much of it has been destroyed by ploughing, but there is still plenty to see, especially to the east of the A354, near Sixpenny Handley. When it was intact, the cursus was a pair of parallel banks 90 yards apart and over six miles long. These banks contained some 6½ million cubic feet of earth and chalk, which must have been loosened using deer horns, scraped on to skins with tools made from shoulder blades and carried by hand. At either end there is a squared enclosure and, outside it, a couple of long barrows. The cursus also encloses a long barrow and incorporates another in one of its banks. It is unlikely to have been a racecourse, as its name suggests, but it might have been a processional way.

While New Stone Age monuments are, for the most part, on the chalk downland, the settlements seem to have been in the river valleys. One such settlement has been excavated near Lodge Farm at Pamphill. Saddle querns were discovered, showing that the people grew cereals, and there were the bones of cattle and pigs.

The first metal to be used for tools was probably copper. Later, this was toughened by adding tin, so creating the alloy bronze. Some Bronze Age civilizations were advanced; the Minoans of Crete, for example, built sumptuous palaces, created marvellous works of art and owned fleets of ships in which they traded over much of the Mediterranean. Bronze Age settlers may have reached Britain in about 2,000 BC. They had a much lower level of culture than the Minoans, but many interesting artefacts have been found, such as daggers, bracelets, necklaces, razors and various kinds of pottery.

The most common of the Bronze Age monuments are the burial mounds known as round barrows. They are of several kinds, the easiest to recognise being the bowl barrow, so named because it is like a bowl turned upside down. Another kind is the disc, which has a low bank and a ditch at some distance from a small central mound. Disc barrows seem to have been for women and bowl barrows for people of either sex. Each round barrow generally held one individual. Many barrows are grouped in cemeteries. There are 17 barrows on the misnamed Nine Barrow Down in Purbeck and there are scores along the Ridgeway, east of the Hardy Monument, but the most impressive cemetery is on Oakley Down, where there are 34 barrows of various kinds. When they were made, barrows were covered with chalk so that they stood out, stark white, in the landscape.

Another kind of Bronze Age monument is the stone circle. There are three such circles in Dorset, at Kingston Russell, Rempstone and Winterbourne Abbas. The first is about 80 feet in diameter, but some of the stones have been removed and all the rest have fallen. The second, which may also have been 80 feet across, has lost most of its stones. The

11

last is the smallest, but is in good condition. It is correctly named Nine Stones, and all are still standing.

A Bronze Age settlement has been excavated at Eldon Seat, on the limestone downs of the Isle of Purbeck, where the inhabitants lived in circular huts. Tools, a silver harness ring and ornaments of Kimmeridge shale were found, as well as bones of farm animals, especially sheep.

The people of the late Bronze Age developed a plough that was drawn by oxen. It gouged a deep furrow, but as it did not turn the sod the land had to be cross ploughed, that is, ploughed from side to side as well as up and down. This led to square shaped plots, traces of which remain in many places. They are known as 'Celtic fields', though many of them pre-date the Celts by centuries.

Migrants of three Iron Age cultures came to Britain, known by their places of origin as Halstatt, La Tène and Belgic. The first wave probably arrived in the eighth century BC, the second in the fourth century BC and the third in about 100 BC. More Belgic people came in 52 BC, fleeing from the Romans.

Dorset and south Somerset were occupied by a tribe known to the Romans as the Durotriges. Their culture was a blend of Halstatt and La Tène, and they seem to have been influenced by the Belgae, though it is unlikely that they were conquered by them.

Many Iron Age artefacts have been discovered. Some are of high quality but few in number, suggesting a tribal aristocracy, and these include bronze mirrors, brooches, fancy harness fittings and some splendid swords. There are many humbler items as well, such as tools and pottery. One of the most remarkable finds was a chain with a very modern looking anchor. It came to light on Bulbury Hill, a most unlikely place for an anchor.

There are many round barrows from the Iron Age, but the most characteristic monuments of the period are the hill forts. There are 31 in Dorset, of different kinds and sizes. The basis of all the defences is the ditch and the bank. Often, there are banks on both sides of the ditch, the one towards the enemy, known as the counterscarp, being the smaller. Sometimes there are quarry scoops inside the defences, which gave material to make the main bank higher. These can be seen on Hod Hill. The simplest entrance was a gap in the banks, with a causeway over the ditch, but at Bindon Hill the banks turn inwards, making a narrow, dangerous approach. The banks were topped with ramparts, also made from spoil, but with vertical faces of either timber or stone.

Early in the first century BC a new weapon was being used in Britain. This was the sling. It did not take long to load, so even a few men could put down a formidable barrage. For the Durotriges, Chesil Bank was an inexhaustible source of ammunition. In answer to the sling, the occupants of some hill forts built one or even two extra lines of defence. In archaeologists' jargon, 'univallate' forts became 'multivallate'. On level ground, the sling had a range of 100 yards, but this was much more when firing down a slope, and much less when firing up. Suppose then, that some attackers break through the outer bank of a multivallate fort. The defenders on the inner banks, with gravity on their side, can bombard them, but the attackers cannot reply. Multivallate forts were further strengthened by making complicated mazes of banks and ditches in front of their entrances.

Two prehistoric sites in Dorset are worth looking at in some detail. They are Maiden Castle and Hengistbury Head.

Maiden Castle was excavated by Sir Mortimer Wheeler between 1934 and 1937. It stands on a prominent, isolated hill to the south of Dorchester. Neolithic people built a causewayed camp here and a bank barrow no less than 587 yards long, though the camp was obliterated by Iron Age works and the barrow is so badly eroded that it is all but invisible. At the east end of the barrow were the bones of a man who had been hacked to pieces in a fearful piece of butchery. These remains, arranged as they were found, are in the Dorset County Museum.

In about 1500 BC the hill was abandoned, the only find from the Bronze Age being a solitary spearhead. Then, in about 300 BC Iron Age people fortified the eastern part of the hill. Judging by their crude pottery, these were rather primitive folk, but they farmed their square 'Celtic' fields, they wove cloth and they wore a few, simple ornaments. The defences were later extended to enclose the whole of the hill. The settlement then covered 45 acres and there were many houses arranged along metalled streets. Grain storage pits have been discovered that were up to eleven feet deep.

Early in the 1st century BC the defences were strengthened by adding two ditches to the south and one to the north. This was in answer to the threat from the sling. The defenders must have used slings themselves, for several ammunition dumps were found, one containing 20,000 stones. The entrances became tangles of banks and ditches, with stone platforms for slingers, while the gates themselves were protected by high limestone walls on either side.

In the 1st century AD the defences were repaired, the streets were remetalled and the old storage pits were replaced by barns. The fortress was at its strongest and best when the Romans invaded in AD 43.

Hengistbury Head has attracted several archaeologists, including Barry Cunliffe, who published his findings in 1978. The Head forms the southern side of Christchurch Harbour. Old Stone Age hunters came here, and Middle Stone Age people made camps. New Stone Age and Bronze Age knives, arrowheads and scrapers have been found, as well as a Bronze Age cemetery of 13 round barrows. In about 500 or 400 BC early Iron Age folk made a permanent settlement. These people were probably farmers, though axes from Brittany and Sicily suggest that they traded over a wide area.

At some stage, the double dykes were built. They ran from sea to sea across the neck of the Head, curving back to prevent outflanking. Today, the outer dyke is full of silt, while over 100 yards of the southern end of the defences have been lost to the sea.

Hengistbury's great days began in about 100 BC when it became an industrial town, perhaps the first in Britain, and a major port. Its people smelted both the Head's own iron ore and imported ores, lead coming from the Mendips and copper and tin from Devon and Cornwall. The lead and some of the copper contained silver, which was extracted, and there may even have been a mint to turn it into coins. The areas that supplied the ores also sent pottery. Other imported minerals were shale from Kimmeridge, which was turned on the lathe to make bracelets, and manganese glass from Europe, which was probably shaped into beads. Pottery may well have been made, as there are suitable local clays.

Hengistbury was well placed for trade. It has an excellent natural harbour and is less than 70 miles from the Cherbourg peninsula, or twelve hours' sailing on a good day. More Italian amphorae have been found here than anywhere else on the coast of Britain, so, presumably, this was the main port of entry for wine. Almost certainly it came through Gaul, avoiding the long journey round Spain. Pottery also came from Europe. Hengistbury exported its own products and, one would suppose, the goods mentioned by the Roman geographer, Strabo. He said, 'Britain produces corn, cattle, gold, silver, iron. All these are exported together with hides, slaves and dogs useful for hunting.'

Hengistbury's main trading partners were the Veneti of Brittany. Caesar described their ships as stoutly built of oak, with leather sails. In 52 BC, though, the tribe made the mistake of rebelling against Caesar, and he virtually destroyed it. Hengistbury's prosperity ended immediately. It sank to no more than a peasant settlement, remaining as such until the end of the Roman occupation. In Saxon times the site was abandoned altogether and Christchurch was built on the other side of the harbour.

2

ROMAN DORSET

The Roman conquest of Britain began in AD 43, during the reign of the Emperor Claudius. Aulus Plautius led the invasion with four legions, each of 5,000 élite infantrymen, and numerous auxiliaries such as cavalry, archers and slingers.

The Romans won a hard fought battle on the Medway, after which Aulus Plautius divided his army into three, meaning to overrun the rest of Britain. The future emperor Vespasian, legate of the Second Legion, was responsible for subduing the south. His biographer, Suetonius, gave a laconic account of the campaign, saying that the general 'fought thirty battles, conquered two very powerful tribes, captured over twenty towns and annexed the Isle of Wight.'

One of the tribes must have been the Durotriges, for there are signs of conflict in Dorset. The Romans made a camp at Lake Farm near Wimborne, established a port at Hamworthy on Poole Harbour, and stormed the hill forts of Spetisbury Rings, Hod Hill and Maiden Castle.

Sir Mortimer Wheeler's excavations showed what happened at Maiden Castle. The Romans mounted their attack on the eastern entrance, the weaker of the two. First, they put down a barrage of heavy arrows from their ballistas. Next, the legionaries advanced, no doubt protecting themselves from hundreds of sling stones by forming a 'testudo' of shields locked over their heads. They could not have kept that formation when they reached the defences, but they fought their way to the gates. They found some huts in the inner ditch which they fired, so it is possible that the smoke gave them a little cover. Finally, they broke through the gates and, their anger at white heat, they massacred men, women and children. After the slaughter they dismantled the defences of the fort and went on their way, leaving the stunned survivors to bury their dead.

At Hod Hill, the Romans also put down a barrage of ballista arrows, which was enough to make the defenders surrender without a fight. Many of the arrows were aimed at a single hut, which might have been

Roman arrow head in backbone of defender of Maiden Castle. (Dorset County Museum)

a shrine. If so, the Romans demonstrated that the god was unable to protect himself, let alone his people.

After they had taken Hod Hill, the Romans built a camp in its north-west corner, where the banks and ditches remain to this day. They make a striking contrast with the Iron Age defences, which were simply a formidable barrier, while the Roman defences were a trap. The diagram shows how it worked. After a few years, the buildings inside the Hod Hill camp were burnt, probably by the garrison as it was leaving.

When the Romans had defeated a tribe, they tried to civilize it. In the Mediterranean, civilized life meant city life, so the Romans gave the Durotriges a brand new capital which they called Durnovaria. We know it as Dorchester. Durnovaria seems to have been founded in about AD 70 which was during the reign of the Emperor Vespasian, the very man who had destroyed Maiden Castle.

Since Durnovaria lies under a modern town it has been impossible to excavate it systematically, but much of interest has come to light and more is being discovered. A pipe trench for example, can be a useful archaeological section.

16

Durnovaria was about 90 acres, which was respectable for a British tribal capital, the others varying from 35 to 240 acres. It is likely that the streets were laid out by military engineers so that they crossed at right angles, forming regular blocks called 'insulae', or islands. The houses that have been uncovered, though, were not well aligned so it seems that it was difficult to teach the Britons tidy habits.

In the centre of Durnovaria there was a forum or market place and, attached to it, a basilica which was both town hall and law courts. They have been found as a result of pipe laying, though not excavated. The public baths, on the other hand, were uncovered but, as the area was needed for a car park, they were buried again. Bathing was a ritual for the Romans, and the baths were also a place to relax at the end of the day, meet friends and play games.

Just outside the town, to the south, was Durnovaria's equivalent of the Colosseum at Rome, an amphitheatre which is still standing and known today as Maumbury Rings. Originally it was a neolithic henge, but the Romans dug out the whole centre to a depth of ten feet and raised the banks with the spoil. The amphitheatre is 330 feet in diameter so it would have been big enough to take the entire population of the town. We can only guess what happened in the arena, though there would almost certainly have been sports, some of them, perhaps, quite innocent. But there might also have been bear and bull baiting, while criminals could have been tortured and executed. The shows were free to ordinary folk, since the members of the tribal council paid for them.

North-west of Durnovaria was an aqueduct. It followed the contours, so there was nothing like the Pont du Gard in France or the marvellous structure in Segovia to carry it over valleys. Today it is full of spoil, showing only as a narrow terrace on the hillsides. Nonetheless, it was remarkable. It was eleven or twelve miles long and keeping the levels right over such a distance was an achievement. On average, the channel

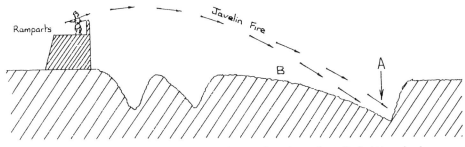

Section through Roman defences on Hod Hill Attackers jump into ditch (A) and advance up gentle slope into killing ground (B). Defenders throw their javelins and attackers are trapped, because they cannot escape up the steep side of the ditch.

was seven feet wide at the top, five feet wide at the bottom and three feet deep. Assuming it held two feet of water, it would have delivered 13 million gallons a day. This would have been fed to the public baths, carried to stand-pipes or fountains in the streets, piped into the wealthier houses and used to scour the sewers, if there were any. Even though the Frome flows right by the town, the aqueduct was useful, for it gave a good head of water. The Romans had pumps, but not with a capacity of 13 million gallons a day.

During work in Colliton Park several houses came to light, one of which has been left on view and is, indeed, the only complete town house of the period to be seen in Britain. The plan is too untidy for pure Roman taste, but that apart, the building shows several classical features such as an arcaded corridor, a hypocaust and several tessellated pavements.

At first Durnovaria was undefended, but in the late 2nd century its people made a massive earth rampart. They then added a stone wall in about AD 300. Only a fragment of the wall remains but tree-lined walks follow most of its course.

Durnovaria must also have been a market centre, where country folk came with their produce and the town's artisans sold their wares. The only signs of these activities that have been uncovered are two furnaces, one for lead and the other for iron. But in other towns there is evidence of butchers, shoemakers, weavers, dyers, farriers, coopers, carpenters and workers in bronze, silver and gold.

Families that owned houses like the one in Colliton Park also had villas. A villa was an isolated country house with Roman characteristics, such as a tiled roof, classical arcades, hypocausts and tessellated pavements. Each villa was the centre of a large farm, so it had barns, stables and workshops. There was a fair sprinkling of villas in Dorset and they have yielded important finds, but none of them is on view.

Ordinary country folk went on living in much the same way as their ancestors had done before the conquest, though there were changes. Roman coins and pottery have been found on many sites indicating trade and an increase in comfort. Rectangular huts were discovered near Studland, which proves there was at least some sophistication. Nature is without rectangles so primitive people have no experience of them and, in consequence, make their buildings round in plan.

One interesting question is whether the Roman conquest brought improvements in agriculture. It is fairly certain that there was an increase in output. The rule was that each province had to feed the troops stationed in it, and Britain had more soldiers for its population than anywhere else in the Empire. Most of the time there were three legions, each consuming 500 bushels of grain a week, and there were many auxiliaries as well. In addition to grain, the soldiers needed meat, fruit and vegetables.

The difficulty is to decide how all this extra food was produced, but there are some clues from a peasant settlement at Woodcutts, on Cranborne Chase. Until about AD 150 there were no changes here, but then three enclosures were made for stock and a well was sunk. It is possible that the inhabitants were overwintering cattle rather than slaughtering most of them, and using the extra manure to improve their yields. It is possible, too, that others were doing the same. All this is conjecture, but there is no doubt about one development. The Romans put an end to tribal warfare and peace is the largest single benefit a farmer can have.

Most craftsmen served their locality, but there were others selling in a wider market. From about AD 120 Dorset potters were supplying large quantities of 'black burnished ware' to the Roman army in the north. A kiln for this work has been discovered at Hamworthy. The industry flourished until AD 367, when the army began ordering from potteries at Malton. There was a trade in articles made from Kimmeridge shale, turned to form bracelets, bowls and platters, as well as carved to form table legs. There was also a thriving business in laying tessellated pavements. This reached its peak in the 4th century, when there were four or five leading schools of mosaicists in Britain, one of them in Durnovaria. The varied geology of the area meant it was easy to find stones of different colours, including Purbeck marble, and to these could be added red tesserae of baked clay. The mosaicists were able to create intricate patterns as well as human, animal and vegetable forms. They could even put an expression on a face. The more complicated parts of a mosaic were assembled in the firm's workshop before being taken to the site.

The Romans are famous for their roads and one of the most important in Britain passed through Dorset. This was the Iter XIV, otherwise known as the Ackling Dyke, which ran from London to Exeter via Old Sarum, Badbury Rings and Dorchester. The Romans knew what Macadam was to rediscover in the 19th century, namely that a road's main enemy is underground water. Accordingly, they built a huge mound, or agger, to raise their road above the level of the surrounding land. There is a marvellous stretch of agger on Oakley Down, where it is between 40 and 50 feet wide and six feet high.

Thanks to the roads, troops and privileged individuals could move quickly and easily, while the Imperial Post could carry a letter from Rome to York in three days. The transport of bulk goods, though, was

Ackling Dyke on Oakley Down.

difficult. It was no more expensive for a ship to carry a cargo of corn the length of the Mediterranean than it was to move the same load 75 miles on land. Much of Britain's traffic must have gone by sea, including the Dorset pottery made for the army. It was when the seas became unsafe that the army began buying its pottery from Malton.

The Romans brought their own gods to Britain but, so far from despising the native deities, they worshipped them. They believed that each area had its own 'genius loci' which it was wise to placate. The Romans were very tolerant in matters of religion, just the Imperial Cult being compulsory; everyone had to worship the spirits of dead emperors as proof of their loyalty to the state. Only Christians refused to do this, so only Christians were persecuted. Then, in AD 312, the Emperor Constantine defeated his rival Maxentus. Constantine was sure the Christian God had helped him, so he made Christianity the official religion of the Empire.

There is not much evidence of early Christianity in Britain as a whole, which means that certain finds in Dorset are especially significant. A mosaic from a villa at Hinton St Mary shows a head, possibly Christ's, while behind it is the Christian Chi-Rho symbol. There is also a large cemetery at Poundbury near Durnovaria where many of the dead were laid east to west and interred without grave goods. These are the marks of Christian burials, so there must have been a large Christian community in the town.

While Christianity was spreading, the old cults still thrived and, again, there is proof of this from Dorset, for in about AD 380 the eastern section of Maiden Castle became a precinct for the worship of pagan gods. The temple's foundations are there to see, along with those of the priest's house. It seems, too, that there were Christians who clung to a few of the old beliefs, for some of the dead in the Durnovaria cemetery were buried with a coin on each eye. Perhaps the relatives felt it would do no harm to make sure that the soul of the deceased could pay Charon to ferry it over the Styx, just in case . . .

Assuming it is Romano-British, as has been suggested, the Cerne Giant must be the most astonishing pagan survival from the period in Britain. There is only speculation as to what, exactly, the figure represents, the Celtic god Nodens being the most likely candidate. Anyone, though, can see that the Giant is a fertility symbol, and the people of Cerne believed in it as such until recent times.

In the later years of the Empire many towns changed their character, for the wealthy ceased visiting them, preferring to live permanently in their villas. At Durnovaria, squatters lit fires on the tessellated pavements

Mosaic of Roman sea god Oceanus, found at Fordington. His beard and his hair are formed from seaweed.

of the Colliton Park house and knocked a hole in one of them to bury a baby.

There were other, far worse, developments. During the 4th century Britain was under attack from Picts, Scots and Saxons and, moreover, by the early 5th century the whole of the western empire was collapsing. The Visigoths sacked Rome itself in AD 410. That same year, the cities of Britain wrote to the Emperor Honorius asking for help and he could only advise them to defend themselves. The 'rescript of Honorius' has been held as marking the end of Roman rule in Britain, but it is unlikely that anyone saw it as such at the time. Life in Durnovaria and the surrounding countryside went on much as before, though all the time the Saxon threat was growing.

3

SAXON DORSET

The Saxons were slow to reach Dorset. Their occupation of Britain was a folk movement spread over many years and it would seem too, that the Britons checked them at the battle of Mount Badon in about AD 500. According to legend, the leader of the Britons was King Arthur and there are suggestions that Mount Badon was Badbury Rings. However, in AD 658 the Saxon King Cenwealh of Wessex won the battle of Penn, at a site now unknown, after which the Saxons occupied Dorset.

In north Dorset there is a bank and ditch known as Bokerley Dyke. It runs across the chalk, blocking the main natural highway into the county. The work dates from the 4th or 5th centuries, so it is tempting to see it as a British line of defence. But there is no serious military value in it, for an enemy with a little determination could have outflanked it, in spite of difficult country at either end. Bokerley Dyke would, though, have hindered cattle raiders. Combs Ditch, about 13 miles to the south-west, is similar to Bokerley Dyke, while the Battery Banks near Wareham may be of the same period.

There is no telling how many Saxons arrived in Dorset, or how many Britons they displaced, but it is certain that numbers of Britons remained. At St Mary's church, Wareham, there are some British inscriptions of the 7th and 8th centuries. Celtic place names survived. Creech means 'hill', Chideock means 'wooded' and Pimperne means 'five trees'. The Dorset river names are Celtic, apart from Piddle and Winterbourne. However, these are all natural features and it is significant that 80 per cent of the towns and villages have Saxon names.

Wherever possible, the Saxons settled in groups, forming nucleated villages. Several families together could defend themselves and reduce the risk of famine by working as a unit. They could share the heavier pieces of equipment, like the ploughs, along with such animals as the draught oxen and the village bull.

The land was held in common, divided into meadow, arable and summer pasture. The meadow would be beside a river or a stream, if there was one. The arable was in fields that were up to a mile across and, with no artificial fertilisers and little dung, they were kept fertile by fallowing. There were usually three fields, one of which was sown in the autumn and one in the spring, to spread the work, while the third lay fallow. Every year the fields changed their uses, allowing each to rest in its turn. They were divided into unenclosed strips, later to be known as 'selions' and which varied in size from a quarter to half an acre, so there could be over 2,000 on a field. The standard holding was 30 acres, or ten to a field. That was 20 or even 40 selions and they were scattered everywhere, all the holdings being intermingled. There were perfectly logical reasons for this, to do with the sharing of equipment, but, unfortunately, there is no space to give them here. The best account is in C. S. Orwin's *The Open Fields*.

The pasture was the uncultivated land which lay beyond the arable. It became known as the 'common'. Stock was driven to it in the morning and returned to the village in the evening.

By the end of the Saxon period most ordinary people were bondsmen of one kind or other. Each one belonged to a lord, known as a thegn, who gave him land and protection. The bondsman in return gave the thegn unpaid service so many days in the week, often with more at certain times of the year. Bondsmen were part of the way towards being slaves, and there were others who were slaves in the full sense of the word. They may have been descendants of Britons.

In about AD 1000, Aelfric, the novices' master at Cerne Abbey, wrote a *Colloquy for exercising boys in speaking Latin*. Various characters are made to talk about their lives, including a ploughman who describes what it was like to be in bondage:

> I have to work far too hard. I go out at dawn driving the oxen to the field and yoke them to the plough. I dare not in the worst weather stay at home for fear of my lord, and when I have yoked the oxen together and fastened the ploughshare to the plough, I have to plough a whole acre or more every day. I have a boy who drives the oxen with a goad and he is also hoarse with the cold and his shouting. Besides that I have to supply the mangers of the oxen with hay and give them water and carry their dung outside. Believe me, it is hard work that I have to perform, for I am not free.

Not every bondsman, though, would have welcomed his freedom, for it would have left him unprotected in a hostile world.

Bokerley Dyke.

The nucleated village with its open fields did not appear everywhere in Dorset. The heaths could not support any concentration of population, so instead of villages there were isolated farms. On the loams of the north and west there were nucleated villages with open fields, but as farmers began clearing the forests from the clays, a patch at a time, they made small, irregular enclosures. This movement however, made little progress in Saxon times.

In any year the people were fortunate if they grew enough to keep themselves alive. They might occasionally produce a small surplus, but it would have been unwise to count on this happening. Consequently, if a village grew into a town it kept its fields and nearly all its inhabitants farmed for at least part of their time. It was not until the 18th century that the towns could rely on the countryside to feed them.

Though some places have come and gone, nearly all our modern towns and villages in Dorset date from Saxon times. The same is true of many boundaries, the county itself being created by the Saxons. Moreover, there are 30 land charters surviving which describe the estate boundaries in such detail that it is sometimes possible to trace them today. For example, an estate at Horton corresponds exactly to the modern parish. It is possible that the Saxons took over British or even Romano-British boundaries.

Even after the battle of Penn brought the Saxons to Dorset, the British kingdom of Dumnonia survived in Cornwall and west Devon, but long before the Saxons conquered it they had to face a new and more dangerous threat from the Vikings.

The first Viking raid on England took place in AD 787 on the Dorset coast, probably at Melcombe Regis. Three ships landed and when a royal official rode from Dorchester to see what the strangers wanted, they killed him. After that there were 40 years' respite, but then the Vikings made sporadic attacks. Most of the raiders were Norwegians, looking for plunder and slaves. They usually made off before the Saxons could gather in strength, though they won a battle on Portland early in the 9th century.

Later, the attacks took a new form. Vikings from Denmark came to England to conquer and settle. They captured York in AD 865 and went on to occupy Northumbria, East Anglia and Mercia. They then attacked Wessex, whose forces were commanded by King Ethelred, and his brothers, the youngest of whom was Alfred. After a gallant resistance, Ethelred was killed in AD 871 at a place known as Marden, which might be Martin, near Cranborne. Alfred now became king of Wessex.

A favourite Danish tactic was to sail as far as possible into the heart of enemy territory and then establish a base from which to ravage the surrounding country. Poole Harbour and the river Frome gave the Danes a highway into Dorset, while Wareham, being the head of navigation, was a good base. In AD 876 the Danes took Wareham, and Alfred, feeling unable to do battle, made peace with them. However, they did not keep their part of the bargain and when the winter was over those who had horses rode for Exeter, while the remainder took to their ships. It seems that they then lost 120 vessels off Swanage. Why that should have happened to such excellent seamen is not at all clear, but the tide can play tricks in this area; sometimes there is a standing wave six feet high on the reef off Peveril Point. It is, though, more likely that the ships were wrecked than that they were defeated in battle, as was once believed.

In AD 879 Alfred overwhelmed the Danes under Guthrum at Edington. The two leaders then made peace, dividing England between them along the line of the Watling Street. Raids from Denmark continued, but Alfred organised his defences. He created a navy, some of whose ships might have been built on Poole Harbour. Probably, he was also responsible for the network of fortresses known as 'burghs'.

Our information about burghs comes from a 16th century transcript of an 11th century document, known as the 'burghal hidage'. It lists the burghs and gives the number of hides, or units of land, attached to each. Dorset had four burghs. Three were certainly Shaftesbury, Christchurch and Wareham, while the fourth was probably Bridport. There is no mention of Dorchester, but it had its Roman walls, and may have already organised its own defence. In general, burghs were no more than 20 miles apart and that is not true of Dorset unless Dorchester is included.

Wareham is unique among the burghs, for not only do its streets follow the Saxon plan, but the earth banks are still intact. This allows us to check one of the theories behind the hidage, namely that each hide should provide one man to defend the local burgh, and that every pole of its walls needed four men. Wareham's walls are 2,200 yards long, which is 400 poles. The town, then, needed 1,600 hides to provide its defenders, which is exactly the figure in the list.

By the time Alfred died, Wessex was secure. His son and grandson, Edward the Elder and Athelstan, conquered the rest of England. That, however, was not the end of the Danish menace and an event at Corfe in AD 978 may well have made England vulnerable. According to legend, King Edward, a boy of 16, was out hunting when he decided to visit his stepmother, Queen Elfrida who was staying at Corfe. A group of servants greeted him, one of whom gave him a cup of wine while another stabbed him in the back. Almost at once, miracles began. The body was thrown down a well, but the well gave off a bright light and ever afterwards its waters had healing powers. When Elfrida decided to bury Edward decently at Wareham, her horse refused to join the funeral procession. After three years at Wareham, the body was still showing no signs of decay. It was then taken to Shaftesbury Abbey, where pilgrims came to the shrine.

Edward's murder meant that Elfrida's son, Ethelred, came to the throne. This accession may have been a disaster for England, since the accounts of Ethelred portray him as weak and indecisive and this was a time when the country needed a resolute king. The Danes began raiding again, in larger numbers than ever. Now, their purpose was to cause damage until they were bribed to leave with vast sums of money, known as 'danegeld'. Hoards of English coins have been discovered in Scandinavia, some of them minted at Bridport.

Again, the Danes took their favourite route into Dorset. They were in Poole Harbour in AD 997–8 and Canute seized Wareham in 1015, from where he ravaged Dorset, Somerset and Wiltshire. Ethelred, known as 'unraed' or 'ill-advised', paid ever increasing sums of danegeld. The troubles ended only when, after Ethelred's death, the Saxon nobles asked Canute to be their king. He was converted to Christianity and, publicly at least, became a model Christian monarch.

At the time of the Saxon invasions many Britons were Christians. They had, though, been out of touch with Rome for a long time, so they had developed their own traditions, as, for example, their way of calculating the date of Easter. The Saxons themselves were pagans, so Celtic missionaries had tried to convert them, at first with some success. Then, in AD 596, Pope Gregory sent St Augustine to Kent, after which Roman Christianity spread. The Anglo-Saxon leaders adopted it as their official religion at the Synod of Whitby in AD 663.

Roman Christianity came to Dorset as a result of persuasion, coercion and conquest. In AD 634 Birinius, the first Bishop of the West Saxons was preaching the importance of baptism. In about AD 690, King Ine of Wessex enforced it with the threat of a 30 shilling fine. Then, as the Saxons conquered more territory, their own religion gained ground at the expense of Celtic Christianity. By the end of the 7th century, the diocese of Ramsbury, now Winchester, had grown too large so, in AD 705, King Ine divided it. Dorset, west Somerset and east Devon became a new diocese, which Ine offered to his kinsman, Aldhelm, Abbot of Malmesbury. Aldhelm built his cathedral at Sherborne.

The new bishop had 'keen eyes, red cheeks, excellent hearing and wonderful hands'. He tried, in his own words, to 'win men's ears and then their souls'. Being 'the best of all lute players and the most finished of singers', he would stand on a bridge, busking, until he had gathered a crowd. He would then preach to them. Six miracles are attributed to Aldhelm, one being that he 'stretched' a beam that had been cut too short, by blessing it. There is a similar story about Christchurch.

Later Bishops of Sherborne had other gifts. Ealstan led an army against the Danes, 'made great slaughter and gained the victory.'

In the early years of Christianity there were few priests and fewer churches, so the Saxons established minsters. A minster was a church with a college of priests that served a wide area. The parishes of Sturminster Marshall, Corfe Mullen, Lytchett Matravers, Lytchett Minster and Hamworthy, for example, may all have been served from Sturminster Marshall. The minster priests went from parish to parish, preaching at stone crosses.

Christchurch may already have had a minster and Athelstan, the grandson of King Alfred, founded another at Milton Abbas. He was there at the start of one of his campaigns against the Danes when he had a dream that, one day, he would become king of all England. He went on to win the victory of Brunanburgh in AD 937, and in his gratitude he founded a minster church in the place where he had had his dream.

In the later Saxon period many parishes acquired their own churches and their own priests. The churches were usually gifts from their thegns.

Several Dorset monasteries were established under the Saxons. Cerne dated from the 9th century, but was refounded as a Benedictine house in AD 987. One of its most famous monks was Aelfric, who had charge of the novices' school in the late 10th century. His *Colloquy for exercising boys in speaking Latin* has already been mentioned. He also translated the first five books of the Old Testament into Anglo-Saxon, for he believed that ordinary folk should have access to the Bible. With even more daring, he denied the doctrine of transubstantiation, saying that the bread and the wine of the communion service were only spiritually the body and blood of Christ. The Protestant reformers of the 16th century quoted Aelfric with approval.

The font at Melbury Bubb is made from a fragment of a cross shaft. It was carved with a bestiary. Here, a lion is eating a dog, as may be seen by looking at the page upside down.

Canute plundered Cerne Abbey when he was a warring Viking, but restored it when he became king of England and a Christian. His chief steward, Orc, founded Abbotsbury monastery in 1026.

Athelstan's minster at Milton Abbas became a Benedictine monastery in AD 964. Sherborne, too, acquired a monastery soon afterwards. Archbishop Dunstan's policy was to appoint monks as bishops, so in AD 998 he gave St Wulfsin a charter to drive out the secular clergy and build a monastery. After that, the cathedral was also an abbey church.

For a religious house to prosper it had to attract pilgrims, so it needed a saint, some miracles and some relics. Sherborne acquired a saint in Wulfsin, for miracles were performed at his tomb. His remains became relics and when his coffin was opened 'a sweet smell came forth'.

Dorset's most important nunnery was at Shaftesbury. King Alfred has had the credit for founding it, but it may have been in existence well before his time. It is certain, though, that he endowed it handsomely and made his daughter Aethelgifu its abbess. Great men sometimes disposed of surplus daughters in this way. Shaftesbury nunnery attracted many pilgrims and gained much wealth after it acquired the remains of King Edward the Martyr.

Wareham had a priory for nuns, founded in about AD 700. It shared the unhappy fate of the town, sacked by the Danes in AD 876 and again, by Canute, in 1015.

At Wimborne, there was a Benedictine house for both monks and nuns, though a strong wall kept them apart. The monastery was founded by Cuthberga, sister of King Ine and the first abbess. On her death, her sister Tetta became abbess. At that time there was a prioress who was hateful to the novices and when she died, the girls danced on her grave. The earth sank several inches, which was hardly surprising, but Tetta saw it as a sign of God's displeasure. She ordered the novices to fast for three days, while she prayed for the soul of the prioress. As Tetta prayed, the soil in the grave rose again to ground level.

In 1013 the Danes destroyed the Wimborne monastery and it was not rebuilt, but in 1043 Edward the Confessor founded a minster there with a college of secular canons.

Religion was important to the Saxon kings, for the state was weak and faced powerful enemies. Something was needed to unite the people and Roman Christianity seemed the answer. Further, the machinery of government was rudimentary, so rulers needed the Church to help them control their subjects. It is perhaps significant that, with the exception of Bridport, all the burghs were important religious centres, making them spiritual as well as military strongholds. The advantages of Christianity to a ruler probably explain Canute's conversion.

In Britain, urban civilization was already decaying during the last years of the Roman Empire. The Saxons killed it outright. It is true that Dorchester remained occupied, probably because of its protecting walls, but lesser places were abandoned entirely. Roman Gillingham, such as it was, stood on a site nearly half a mile from the Saxon settlement. Later, the Saxons built towns of their own. They were needed for markets and trade, and kings encouraged them by granting them mints; at one stage Shaftesbury had three.

A town gained if it became a burgh or acquired a religious house. Wareham enjoyed several advantages, for it was at the head of navigation of Poole Harbour and the river Frome, it was a burgh and it had a nunnery. It was one of the most important towns of Saxon Dorset.

4

THE NORMANS

In 1066, Duke William of Normandy defeated the Saxons under King Harold at Hastings. The battle was only the start of a bitter war during which the north of England was devastated, but by 1071 the Normans were the masters of the whole of England.

After the Conquest, nearly all the Saxon thegns lost their estates to Normans. Distributing the land was an enormous task, and when it was over William ordered a survey. He wanted to be sure that each of his followers had the lands to which he was entitled, and he wanted to know what taxes he could levy. The survey was likened to the Last Judgement, so it became known as Domesday Book. It was completed in 1086, having taken barely a year.

Domesday Book gives much information but, unfortunately, it is not easy to interpret. Consider two entries for Dorset:

Robert also holds Leigh. Two thegns held it in the time of King Edward. It paid tax for one hide. Land for 1 plough.
3 villeins have it there.
Meadow, 2 acres; woodland 1 furlong long and 5 rods wide.
The value was 13 shillings; now 20 shillings.

Edward also holds Kinson. Wulfwen held it in the time of King Edward. It paid tax for 13 hides. Land for 9 ploughs of which 5 hides and 1 virgate of land are in demesne; 2 ploughs there; 7 slaves.
18 villeins, 14 cottars and 4 coscets, with 7 ploughs.
A mill which pays 5 shillings; woodland, 1 acre; meadow 100 acres less 5; pasture 3 leagues long and 2 leagues wide, less 3 furlongs.
Value of these two manors [Canford and Kinson] when he acquired them £50; now £70.

Here, then, is a great deal about these two places. The trouble begins when we try to extract specific information. For a start, none of the

Chancel arch at Worth Matravers. The arch is decorated with zig-zag, a typical Norman motif.

measures is standard. We believe, for example, that a virgate was sometimes about 30 acres and that a hide was four virgates, but this is hardly the basis for accurate statistics. What is a plough land? Obviously, it is an area of land that can be cultivated with one plough but it is not clear what that was in acres. In any event, we would expect plough lands to vary in size, depending on the soil. Further, there is no mention of pasture at Leigh. It is hard to see how farmers could manage without summer pasture for their stock. Was there really none at Leigh, or has it been left out in error? Indeed, pasture is missing from a quarter of all the Dorset entries, and it is incredible that so many villages should have been without.

A further complication is that much of west Dorset is covered by what is known as the Exeter Domesday. This is much more detailed than Domesday proper giving, for example, far more figures for livestock. It may have been one of the preliminary surveys from which the final account was compiled. We have then, two sets of figures and we would expect the one to supplement the other. However, there are so many discrepancies that the Exeter Domesday only adds to the confusion.

Despite its limitations, however, Domesday does allow us to compare Dorset's natural regions: the down, the vale and the heath.

On the heath, Domesday shows a scattering of little settlements beside the rivers, a population density of 3.5 families to the square mile, few plough teams and few mills.

On the chalk down, the settlements were, again, along the river valleys. They were, though, fairly large nucleated villages on adequate deposits of loam and there was a population density of 8.5 families to the square mile. There were numerous plough teams and mills. While the higher levels of the chalk did not attract settlements, they were valuable grazing for sheep. There were already some flocks of over 1,000.

In the vale the colonisation of the clays had hardly begun, though they were valuable since they were covered with broad-leaved trees and yielded timber and firewood. Moreover, there were many square miles of loam, so that overall the population density was about the same as on the chalk. Again, there were plenty of plough teams and mills. As would be expected, sheep were far fewer, the exception being the Isle of Portland and a tract of land to the north-west of it, extending some eight miles to Abbotsbury.

Domesday also allows us to make at least some tentative comparisons between Dorset and the other counties of England. Dorset had a rural population with a density of 7.5 recorded persons per square mile, which was only just above the national average, and well below the Suffolk figure of 13.1. But when annual values are measured in shillings per square mile, Dorset is in fourth place with 68, the national average being 32. Moreover, Dorset moves into first place when annual values are measured in shillings per plough team, the county's figure being 33, or nearly double the national average. When it comes to mills, Dorset is again in first place, with 147 for every 1000 teams, and 43 per 1000 of recorded population. The national averages are 75 and 25 respectively.

These figures suggest that Dorset was one of the most prosperous counties of England and that is was producing, for its plough teams and population, more grain than any other.

While the Dorset countryside seems to have survived the Norman Conquest more or less intact, the fate of the towns was very different. Domesday mentions five boroughs, or important towns, though we have to infer the existence of Wimborne from rural entries. The other four boroughs have their own entries, which tell a dismal story. Hugh Fitz Grip was the first Norman Sheriff of Dorset:

> In Dorchester in the time of King Edward there were 172 houses. Now there are 88 houses there; 100 have been completely destroyed from the time of Hugh the Sheriff until now.

> In Bridport in the time of King Edward there were 120 houses. Now there are 100 houses there; 20 are derelict.

> In Wareham in the time of King Edward there were 143 houses in the king's demesne. Now there are 70 houses there; 73 have been completely destroyed from the time of Hugh the Sheriff. In St Wandrille's part there are 45 houses standing and 17 are derelict. In the other barons' parts there are 20 houses and 60 have been destroyed.

> In the Borough of Shaftesbury in the time of King Edward there were 104 houses in the king's demesne. Now there are 66 houses there; 38 houses have been destroyed from the time of Hugh the Sheriff until now. In the Abbess's part there were 153 houses in the time of King Edward. Now there are 111 houses there; 42 have been entirely destroyed. The abbess has 20 empty dwellings.

The reasons for this devastation are not known. At Dorchester, Wareham and Shaftesbury the Normans built castles, for which they had to make room, but it cannot have been necessary to destroy so many houses. Wareham lost half its houses, but the castle took up, at the most, a tenth of the town. A better explanation might be a rising at Exeter in 1169,

Studland church.

Above: Detail of chancel arch, Studland.

Left: Detail of corbel table, Studland. This corbel table may show pagan influence. Horses, for example, were sacred to the Celts. The sculptor, though, has kept these symbols outside the church.

36

whose leaders tried to form a league of towns. It is possible that the Dorset boroughs co-operated and that the damage was their punishment. All is surmise. Once again, Domesday has given us, simultaneously, much useful information and an unsolved problem.

It is ironic that the Normans should have destroyed so much in the towns, for they have a reputation for being zealous builders. They did, indeed, build a great deal in Dorset, starting with castles for themselves.

When a Norman baron took over his estates he and his few followers wanted protection quickly and their likely answer was to build an earth and timber castle known as a 'motte and bailey'. The motte was a truncated cone, capped with a stockade and a hall for the lord, his family and close retainers. The bailey was lower than the motte, but covered a wider area. On it there were, for example, living quarters for the armed followers, stables and a kitchen. There were numbers of motte and bailey castles in Dorset and one with both mounds intact lies hidden in woodland near Cranborne. Elsewhere the baileys have disappeared but there are several mottes, the most accessible being at Christchurch and Shaftesbury. At Corfe, the Normans had a ready made motte and bailey in the top of the hill, which has two levels.

As soon as they could, the Normans replaced their wooden walls with stone. Sometimes they simply ringed the top of the motte with a wall, so making a 'shell keep', as at Windsor. There are no shell keeps in Dorset, though at Christchurch, Baldwin de Redvers built a square keep on the motte. His only concession to the shape of the motte was to bevel the corners of the keep. It was more common, though, to abandon a motte and bailey castle, because the mounds would not stand the weight of the new stone walls. There was no such problem at Corfe, where the early 12th century saw the beginnings of one of the most powerful castles in England. The Normans fortified the topmost knoll with a stone curtain wall and inside it they built a towering square keep.

Corfe was a royal fortress. The only baronial castle with substantial ruins still standing is Sherborne. After the Conquest, William I made Osmund of Seez Bishop of Salisbury and endowed his cathedral with lands that included Sherborne. Osmund protected these lands by decreeing that anyone who took them from the Church 'should be accursed in this world and the next.' Early in the 12th century another bishop, Roger of Caen, took more practical defensive measures by building Sherborne Castle. This consisted of a central block, surrounded by a curtain wall. The central block was in two parts, a tower keep, rather like Corfe, and a palace built round a courtyard. The curtain has three gateways, one of them protected by a barbican. There are also two fairly insignificant wall towers. In later centuries any curtain would

Nave arcade of Christchurch Priory.

have had numerous projecting towers so that defenders could cover the base of the walls. In the 12th century, though, such towers were hardly necessary, because siege craft was still quite primitive.

While the Normans built castles for security in this life, they built churches to ensure a comfortable existence in the next. Since they thought the Saxon churches were crude, they demolished most of them. The religious houses of Abbotsbury, Cerne, Christchurch, Milton, Shaftesbury and Sherborne were all rebuilt lavishly. Parish churches were rebuilt as well. The only Saxon church in Dorset with its walls largely intact is St Martin's at Wareham and even here the chancel arch, a curious hybrid, looks more Norman than Saxon. The principal church of Wareham, St Mary's, also survived the Normans, but not the Victorians, who demolished it 'on the grounds that the oratorical qualities of the rector deserved a better setting.'

As well as replacing existing churches the Normans built new ones, for they wanted every parish to have its own church and priest. It is unlikely that they achieved this ambition, but they went a long way towards it.

The Normans built so vigorously that there are fragments of their work all over the county. Moreover, there are several almost complete Norman churches, including Studland and Worth Matravers, though the most striking Norman monument is the superb nave of Christchurch Priory. After the Conquest the manor came into the hands of Ranulf Flambard, who decided to replace the Saxon minster with an Augustinian priory. Ranulf was Bishop of Durham and was responsible for building the magnificent cathedral in that town. Clearly, he insisted that the work at Christchurch should be of the same high standard.

There is a legend about the building of the priory at Christchurch, a place known to the Saxons as Twynham. It had been decided to put the priory on St Catherine's Hill, about two miles from the Saxon church, but every night the building materials that had been assembled on the hill were spirited away back to the old site. Obviously, that was where the priory had to be built. When operations began the workers were joined by a man who toiled with them, but neither lived with them nor drew any pay. Then a vital beam was cut too short and everyone ended the day in despair. The next morning, though, they found to their joy that the beam had grown to its correct length. The identity of the mysterious workman now seemed clear, and Twynham was given a new name.

5

THE MEDIEVAL COUNTRYSIDE

During the Middle Ages there were baronial wars from time to time, but they did not bring the widespread destruction that the Danes had once caused. For close on 300 years after the Norman Conquest much of Dorset was, relatively speaking, undisturbed and as a result it prospered.

The population grew. There is evidence for this in early 13th century tax lists known as Subsidy Rolls, which give the people assessed. They are no clear guide to the actual population, because a great many folk evaded payment, but they do indicate trends. For the hamlet of Monkton Up Wimborne, Domesday lists nine heads of households, while the Subsidy Roll of 1332 gives 17 tax payers. It is reasonable to suppose, then, that the population of the hamlet had increased considerably.

The growth in population meant an increase in the size and number of settlements, a development which took different forms on the heath, on the down and in the vale.

On the heath, more and more isolated farms appeared, each with its small, enclosed fields. Inevitably, they were confined to the traditional areas, that is the river valleys and the fringes of the heath, while the heath proper was still used only for gathering fuel and for rough grazing.

On the down, the settlements were also limited to their traditional areas, the narrow river valleys. The villages spread along the valley, though, so that they met, creating a kind of medieval ribbon development. At the same time the people brought more land into cultivation by increasing the size of the open fields. There must have been land hunger, for many of the steep slopes of the chalk were ploughed. This was only made possible by the enormous labour of cutting terraces, known as 'strip lynchets'. Also, documents sometimes mention 'pastures several throughout the year', which indicates enclosures. Probably, they were made for sheep, on the tops of the downs.

In the vale, developments on the sandstones and limestones followed much the same pattern as on the chalk, with villages growing bigger

Strip lynchets on Portesham Down. This photograph shows the immense amount of work that was needed to create strip lynchets.

and adding to their open fields. In addition, the colonisation of the clays began, but isolated farms appeared, rather than nucleated villages. The people wrested small, irregular patches of land from the forest, which they enclosed. Many of the farm names end in 'hay', such as Bluntshay, Revelshay and Sminhay. 'Hay' means 'enclosure', while the prefix is usually a personal name. Narrow, deep, winding lanes linked the little settlements, and still do.

Much of Dorset was given over to the royal forests of Gillingham, Blackmoor and Powerstock. A forest was a tract of land set aside for the king's deer. People were allowed to settle in it, though they had to respect 'vert and venison'. That meant they must not disturb any of the vegetation on which the deer fed, that they might not take any of the deer and that in times of shortage the deer had priority over farm animals. The forests provided the king with hunting and his household with fresh meat during the winter. The forest courts were also a useful source of income, for they could inflict any punishment from a fine to the death sentence with confiscation of property.

In the north of Dorset was Cranborne Chase, which extended from Wimborne to Salisbury and from Shaftesbury to Ringwood. With a circuit of 80 miles, it covered a quarter of a million acres. It was a deer preserve, though the chase courts had far fewer powers than the forest courts.

Tower of Bradford Abbas church. Like the manor houses, sumptuous churches are proof of wealth, probably gained in the wool trade.

Lesser nobles had deer parks, where the deer were confined by a bank with a fence and a deep internal ditch. A few of the animals were released into the countryside whenever their owner wanted to hunt. The best preserved of these parks is Harbin's at Tarrant Gunville.

In his *Ancient Law*, 1861, Sir Henry Maine propounded the theory that societies progress from status to contract. Among primitive people relationships depend on status, as between master and slave, while among more advanced people relationships depend on contract, as between employer and employee. During the Middle Ages many people were already making contracts, but status was still important.

At the apex of the social pyramid was the king, the ultimate owner of all the land. The nobles held estates from him, giving services in return. Usually this was 'knight service', that is providing knights to fight in the king's wars for 40 days in each year. Some services, though, were nominal. The Earle family, for example, held Charlborough 'by service of pouring water on the King's hands on Easter or Christmas Day', and Nichola, wife of Nicholas de Morteshore held Abbotsbury 'by service of counting the King's chessmen and putting them in the box when the King had done playing with them.'

At the level of the village there were the lord and his bondsmen. The lord kept a farm to provide for his household which was known as his 'demesne'. The rest of the land was distributed among the bondsmen who, in return, worked on the demesne without payment. Here, for example, are the services of Robert Tac of Marnhull. He ploughed for two days in the winter and for one day in the summer, using his own plough and oxen. At certain times he weeded the lord's corn and helped mow the lord's meadow. He worked five days a week from the end of June to the end of September, helping with the harvest.

It might be wondered how Robert could be spared from his own farm at the busiest time of the year, but he was probably the head of an extended family, with several young men to help him. Only one of them had to work on the lord's demesne.

As a bondsman, Robert could not leave the manor, he could not give his daughter in marriage without licence and when he died, his heir would have to pay a heriot to the lord, perhaps his best beast, before taking over the farm.

Though he was a bondsman, Robert was not a slave, which meant he had rights. He was entitled to bread, meat, pottage and beer when he did the winter ploughing, he ate his Christmas dinner in the lord's hall, provided he brought a faggot for the cooking, and he could cut timber and feed his pigs in the lord's wood. Most important of all, he held a farm of 30 acres, with use of the common pasture.

Here, then, was an arrangement based on the relative status of lord and bondsman. However, Robert Tac also paid a money rent of six shillings a year. This was a modest step towards a tenancy based on a contract freely negotiated by both parties.

There were numerous slaves in Dorset in 1086, but within a hundred years the class had vanished. The Normans thought that the manumission of slaves was a religious duty, besides which slaves had to be fed, housed and clothed, while bondsmen fended for themselves.

In 1348 there was an invasion of England that was far worse than foreign armies. A ship arrived at Melcombe Regis bringing the bubonic plague, or Black Death. This disease was caused by the microbe *Pasteurella pestis* which infected a flea that was carried by the black rat. Normally, the flea bit only its host, but when suffering from the plague it would bite anything, including humans. The numbers of ordinary folk who died are not recorded, but there are figures for the clergy. Normally, one parish priest was instituted in Dorset in any month, but during the seven months after the arrival of the plague, 100 were instituted. Winterborne Clenston lost four priests in just six months. From this information it is difficult to decide on a figure for the population as a whole, but it is possible that between a third and a half of the people died. Nor was 1348 the end, for the plague returned from time to time until the 1660s.

So many people died that the amount of land under cultivation shrank considerably and, indeed, whole villages were abandoned. But a use was found for the empty fields, which were enclosed and turned into pasture for sheep, so that only a solitary shepherd was needed where several ploughmen had once worked. If the returns for the clergy are correct, the plague was worse on the chalk than elsewhere in the county. Why that should have been is a mystery, but the result was to give extra encouragement to sheep rearing in the very region where it was likely to be most profitable. It is at least possible, then, that one result of the Black Death was to enrich the landowners. Certainly, Dorset has several fine manor houses that are evidence of this.

There were changes, too, for humbler folk. Bondsmen's services became much more of a burden. As we have seen, Robert Tac of Marnhull owed five days work every week during harvest time. He could meet this easily enough, provided there were several men in his family. But if the plague meant that only one was left, then having to give the five days' work was an intolerable burden. Since labour was short, there were plenty of landowners who would pay good wages to attract workers. A bondsman, though, could not leave his village, so here was another reason to be frustrated. For the first time it was an advantage to

Priest's door, Bradford Abbas.

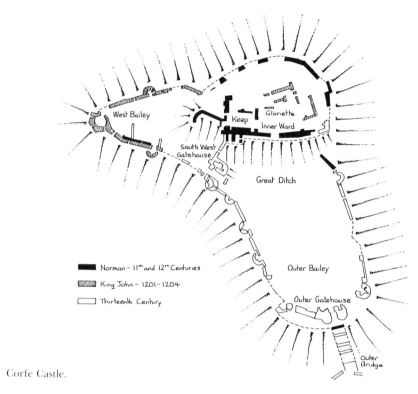

Corfe Castle.

Legend:
- Norman – 11th and 12th Centuries
- King John – 1201–1204
- Thirteenth Century

Labels on plan: West Bailey, Keep, Gloriette, Inner Ward, South West Gatehouse, Great Ditch, Outer Bailey, Outer Gatehouse, Outer Bridge

Corfe Castle from the east. The ruins of the Norman keep dominate. Just to the right of it are the remains of John's 'Gloriette'. Stephen's motte and bailey castle, 'The Rings', can be seen in front of the wood, in the middle distance. The Roundheads damaged Corfe beyond repair, after they captured it in the Civil War. (See also page 107)

46

be free, which was one of the reasons for the Peasants' Revolt of 1381. It did not spread to Dorset, though even here there must have been much sullen, dumb resistance. At first the lords tried to enforce their dues, but in the end they realised it was better to employ paid workers than to extract services from unwilling bondsmen.

By the early 16th century there were few bondsmen left in Dorset. They had commuted their services for money rents and held their land by virtue of entries copied into the rolls of the manor courts. This tenure, known as 'copyhold', was almost as good as freehold and, moreover, it could be bought and sold. Thus, while the Norman period saw the end of slavery, the later Middle Ages saw the end of bondage. Status gave place to contract, and a modern society was born.

Mention must be made of Dorset's two most important medieval castles, Corfe and Sherborne. At Corfe, the Normans had fortified the topmost knoll, or inner ward, and built a keep on it. King John, wanting more luxury than the keep could offer, built a hall alongside it called the 'Gloriette'. The castle was now as much a royal palace as a fortress. But John also strengthened the defences, for he walled the lower part of the hill top, so creating the west bailey, and he dug the Great Ditch along the south side of the inner ward. An even more ambitious campaign began soon afterwards in the reign of Henry III, when the lower slopes of the hill were fortified to make the Outer Bailey. Entry was through a gatehouse of two massive towers, with a drawbridge, and there was a similar gatehouse between the Outer and West Baileys. The walls were strong, and made even stronger by powerful drum towers, set at close intervals. This was the style which Edward I was to use for the impregnable castles that he built in the late 13th century, to hold down the Welsh.

During the earlier anarchy of King Stephen's reign (1135–1154), Corfe had been held by Baldwin de Redvers, a supporter of the rival for the throne, Matilda. Stephen besieged the castle, without success, in 1138 and 1139. As his base he constructed a motte and bailey castle, which is still just visible and is known as 'the Rings'. Apart from these two sieges, Corfe saw little fighting during the Middle Ages. It did, though, gain notoriety, thanks to King John.

John was probably no worse than many other medieval kings, but he fell out with the Church and the monkish chroniclers of his day gave him a bad press. Events at Corfe did nothing for his reputation. From the beginning of his reign in 1199 he had a rival for the throne in his nephew, Prince Arthur of Brittany. In the course of fighting in France, John captured 25 knights whom he brought to Corfe. They lived there in tolerable comfort, until they seized the keep and tried

47

to take the whole castle. John then flung 22 of them into a dungeon, leaving them to starve. Later, John captured Arthur in France and murdered him, for which he was denounced by William de Braose. John imprisoned de Braose's wife and son in Corfe where they also starved to death. Yet another prisoner in Corfe was Arthur's younger sister, Eleanor, the 'Rose of Brittany'. She was allowed royal companions, the princesses Margery and Isabel, who were the daughters of the King of Scotland. The Exchequer accounts show these ladies were paid a regular allowance and from time to time received gifts of luxurious clothes, such as fur-lined capes and fine linen. Eleanor was also given saddles and reins, so she must have been allowed to go riding.

Sherborne Castle, it will be remembered, was protected by the curse of Bishop Osmund of Seez, which threatened dire consequences for anyone who dared to take it from the Church. King Stephen defied the curse, and his reign could hardly have been more troubled. He kept his throne but his rival, Matilda, humbled him and he had to accept her son as his successor. Later, several Earls of Salisbury held the castle. One was beheaded, one lost an eye and another killed his son by accident. The fourth Earl was especially unfortunate. He was among the most successful English generals in the Hundred Years War, and in 1428 he laid siege to Orleans. Legend has it that during a lull in the fighting a boy was wandering round the battlements when he found a cannon that had been left by its crew, who had gone to eat. The cannon was loaded and the boy could not resist firing it. His chance shot killed the Earl of Salisbury. For a time, Sherborne Castle reverted to the Church but, as we shall see, Walter Raleigh obtained it by guile. He was executed on the orders of James I. James gave the castle to his eldest son Henry, who died within the year. After that the curse ran out of steam, for the Digby family has held the castle ever since, with no ill effects.

THE MEDIEVAL TOWNS

Dorset's towns were in a desperate state after the Norman Conquest, but they grew and prospered during the early Middle Ages. In the later Middle Ages, they must have suffered even more than the villages from the Black Death. There are no contemporary descriptions, but we can imagine tolling bells, deserted streets, silent workshops and empty ships moored in the harbours. Evidence for what followed is contradictory. Dorchester and Poole, for example, seem to have flourished in the 15th century while other places, such as Lyme Regis, Melcombe Regis and Weymouth stagnated.

Most towns began as villages, so each had its lord and the inhabitants were bondsmen. But if a village grew into a town, it sought privileges, which would be granted by charters from the lord or from the crown. One of the first steps was to become a borough, which meant that the citizens were no longer bondsmen but free burgesses, paying money rents to their lord rather than giving him manorial services. The next stage was to escape from the control of the manorial court so that the town was governed by a group of its burgesses, headed by a port reeve or mayor. The existence of a mayor was usually a sign that a town was managing its own affairs. The Crown might help by granting the rights to form a merchant guild and to hold markets and fairs. The different Dorset towns went different distances along this road, with Poole in the lead.

All Dorset towns had two things in common. In the first place, they remained to quite an extent rural communities, each with its common fields. Most of the inhabitants were part time or even full time farmers. Secondly, they all had craft industries and were market centres, even if they did not have the formal right to hold markets on stated days. Their people might grow much of their own food, but they still had to buy from the surrounding countryside. In exchange, they offered the goods that they made in their workshops, such as pottery, farm tools, cloth and footwear. Apart from these two factors, however, there were many differences between them.

The Pitchmarket, Cerne Abbas. Terrace of houses from one of Dorset's smaller medieval towns.

Blandford seems to have owed its existence solely to its market. Domesday mentions five Blandfords, but it is clear that they were all villages and hamlets, so the town must have appeared during the Middle Ages. It was well positioned, for it stood where several roads met at a crossing of the river Stour. After the place had grown it was decided to show the importance of its trade by adding Forum, the Latin word for 'market', to its name.

Several Dorset towns grew up alongside monasteries. The Cistercians did not welcome neighbours, but the Benedictines liked to have towns close at hand. The inhabitants provided services and the monks could collect rents, fines and market tolls. As for the townsfolk, they found that the monasteries with their numerous inmates, their wealth and their pilgrims were good for business. Sherborne, Christchurch, Cerne Abbas, Abbotsbury, Middleton (Milton Abbas) and, to a lesser extent, Cranborne, all thrived. At Shaftesbury, the site of the Saxon burgh was inconvenient, being a narrow spur, so a new town was built where roads met just to the north-east of the nunnery.

A castle could encourage the growth of a town in much the same way as a monastery, as happened at Corfe. Christchurch had both a castle and a priory.

Another stimulus to towns, though less usual, was the manufacture of goods that were sold outside the immediate area. Only three Dorset towns developed such industries, Bridport, Corfe and Dorchester.

The loams which cover the limestones around Bridport are good for hemp and flax, so farmers grew these crops and the townsfolk turned the fibres into ropes and nets. In 1213, King John sent the following message to the Sheriff of Dorset:

> We command you that as you love us, yourselves and your own body that you cause to be made at Bridport, night and day, as many ropes for ships, both large and small, and as many cables as you can, and twisted yarns for cordage for ballistas.

In 1253, Henry III gave Bridport a charter, making it a royal borough.

Corfe's industry was the quarrying and shaping of Purbeck marble. This is not a true marble, but a limestone which consists of the shells of freshwater snails in a coloured matrix. It can be green, red, blue or black. The stone takes a high polish, but it does not withstand the weather, so it was always used indoors.

Purbeck marble was especially popular in the 13th century, when the Early English style of church architecture was in fashion. Master masons liked to put clusters of detached shafts of it round their columns. There are fine examples of this treatment at Lincoln and Salisbury.

Fonts, altar tables, bases for memorial brasses and effigies were also made from Purbeck marble. The effigies are rather flat, so they fail to do justice to hooked noses and ample bosoms. This may have been because the seams of marble were narrow, but it was more likely the result of artistic style. The earliest effigy in Purbeck marble is of Leofric, Bishop of Exeter, who died in 1072. The earliest royal effigy is King John's, in Worcester Cathedral. It was carved in 1240.

During the later Middle Ages the style for church columns was a cluster of attached shafts, all of the same stone, while alabaster was favoured for effigies. As a result, the Purbeck industry declined. However, at the time of writing the Company of Marblers still exists. Every Shrove Tuesday, until recently, its members kicked a football over the heath and into Poole Harbour at Ower. They then sprinkled a pound of pepper over it. They did this in memory of an agreement their ancestors made with the landowner, which was to pay him a football and a pound of pepper every year, in exchange for the right of way.

The third town that developed an important industry was Dorchester. At first, nearly all the raw wool produced in England was exported, but from the 14th century onwards more and more of it was spun and woven at home. Dorchester, being at the heart of a major sheep rearing area, became one of the centres of the new industry. St Peter's church is some evidence of the town's prosperity, for it was rebuilt early in the 15th century. Dorchester was granted a charter by Edward III in 1337.

Numbers of medieval English towns were created by feudal lords, who hoped to collect rents from their burgesses. There were several such schemes in Dorset. In 1286 Edward I ordered the creation of Newton, on the south side of Poole harbour, but nothing happened, and all that remains of the project are names on the map. At Sherborne, in 1227, the Bishop of Salisbury founded the borough of Newlands just beside the old town. It is now part of the main town and there is no way of distinguishing it. There was a similar development at Wimborne. Around the Minster is a maze of little streets. They made up the old town, which belonged to the Minster. Just north of this area are two streets, East Borough and West Borough. They run parallel to each other, and certainly look the result of planning. They did not belong to the Minster, but to the lord of the manor of Kingston Lacy, who must have added his own borough to the one already existing. Both boroughs held markets, which competed with each other.

Dorset's coastal towns owed a great deal to the marriage of Henry II and Eleanor of Aquitaine in 1152. From then and for almost exactly 300 years, England and south-west France were under the same rulers. The one region produced wool and the other wine, so there was much trade between them. Dorset took its share.

In 1086 Lyme Regis had been a small fishing village, with a salt works. In those days Axe Haven was a port of some consequence, and Lyme could offer ships no protection at all. Then, in the 13th century, the mouth of the Axe was blocked, perhaps by a cliff fall or perhaps by a shingle bar. The people of Lyme Regis seized this opportunity and built a breakwater, known as the Cobb. It was two parallel rows of oak piles, the space between them filled with cowstone boulders. These were floated between barrels from the beach at Dowlands, over three miles to the west. The Cobb is first mentioned in 1295 and it may be significant that in 1284 Lyme had secured a royal charter making it a free borough and granting it a merchant guild.

The builders of the Cobb knew that it could act like a groyne, with shingle piling up on its west side while it was swept away from the east, exposing the town to the sea. The answer was to leave a gap between the Cobb and the shore, so that the shingle could pass through freely. Unfortunately it blocked the mouth of the river Lim, which acted as the town sewer, but that was the lesser of two evils.

Lyme, though, failed to prosper. From time to time Atlantic gales damaged the Cobb, while in 1337 a storm destroyed it along with some

80 houses and 50 vessels. The French were another danger and it would seem that their raids dampened the prosperity of the town in the 15th century. The plague may also have been partly to blame.

Bridport, in spite of its name, never received any shipping. The suffix 'port' often means 'town' and probably does so here. When vessels were small they could make their way for a short distance up the Brit, but in 1274 a harbour was built at West Bay, on the mouth of the river. Keeping this harbour open was a constant battle, for the river carried silt into it while the sea swept shingle across its mouth.

When coming from the west, the first natural haven on the Dorset coast is Lake Radipole at the mouth of the river Wey. The Romans built a port at Radipole which remained the head of navigation until ships grew too large to reach it. Then, in the 13th century, two towns appeared where the lake disgorges into the sea. To the north of the channel was Melcombe Regis and to the south was Weymouth. Weymouth secured a charter in 1252 and Melcombe Regis in 1280. Both towns shared the harbour which lay between them, and they bickered constantly.

In 1364 Melcombe Regis became a Port of the Staple, which meant it was one of the places that was allowed to export wool. Indeed, both Melcombe and Weymouth should have prospered, since they served a good hinterland that included the best sheep-rearing areas of Dorset as well as the county town. Moreover they had a good harbour, while beyond it lay a magnificent roadstead protected by Chesil Beach and the Isle of Portland. Yet in 1433 the Staple was transferred to Poole, and when the king's antiquary John Leland visited Melcombe in about 1540 he reported, 'the towne as is evidently seene, hath beene far bigger than it is now.' Perhaps, again, French raids and the plague were the causes.

We come now to Poole, Dorset's medieval prodigy. The place is not mentioned in Domesday Book and the land which was to become its site was part of the manor of Canford. Ships sailed to Wareham which, being the head of navigation, was the most important town of the area. But as ships increased in size, and as silt gathered in the Frome, so Wareham lost its advantages. There was, though, a peninsula jutting into the main harbour and flanked by the narrow channel that led into Holes Bay. The tidal water which was funnelled into the channel kept it scoured, so here was the ideal place to build a quay. This happened and Poole was born. Quite when the town first appeared, we do not know, but it was included in a list of 1224 giving the principal ports of England.

Poole's first charter was granted by William Longespée, lord of the manor of Canford, the likely date being 1248. Longespée wanted to go on a crusade, so he was willing to trade privileges for money. The charter shows that Poole had already gained a great deal, for it mentions

Poole's Woolhouse, now a museum. This warehouse was much longer until Thames Street was cut through it in the nineteenth century.

'free citizens or burgesses'. Other privileges were now granted. The burgesses might choose six of their number to govern the town, while the lord of the manor selected one of the six to be port reeve. In addition, the lord's bailiffs would come to Poole to hold a manorial court, which would save the burgesses a five mile journey to Canford. Finally, the lord confirmed the right of the burgesses to graze their stock and gather fuel on his heaths. For their part, the burgesses agreed to pay the lord the sum of 70 marks. The mark was not a coin, but a unit of account worth 16s 8d, or two thirds of a pound. Thus 70 marks were £46 16s 8d. Assuming the burgesses paid in silver pennies, their total weight would have been 46lbs.

In 1249, and having pocketed his 70 marks, William Longespée went on his crusade. In 1250, he was killed leading the English army at the battle of Mansoura in Egypt.

Step by step, and over the centuries, the burgesses of Poole increased their powers. In 1312 the lord of the manor commuted his dues for a fixed annual payment of 13 marks. In 1364 the Winchelsea Certificate, granted by the crown, recognised Poole's rights over its harbour and a stretch of the open sea beyond it. It was given an admiralty court, over which the mayor presided as admiral of the port. Incidentally, this certificate is the first document to mention the office of Mayor of Poole.

In 1433 a royal charter raised the status of Poole from 'creek' to Port of the Staple, which, as we have seen, displaced Melcombe Regis. One of Poole's oldest buildings, the Town Cellars, dates from this period. It was often referred to as the 'Woolhouse', so it is likely that it was built after the granting of the 1433 charter. In the same year, the town was given a licence to fortify itself and the burgesses cut off their peninsula with a wall and a ditch, as well as building a wall along the sea front.

Twenty years later another royal charter granted a Thursday market and two fairs a year. To regulate the markets and fairs there was a Court of Pie Powder. This expression was the best that Englishmen of the day could make of 'pieds poudrés', which referred to the state of the shoes of the tradesmen who brought their goods along the medieval roads.

It would seem, then, that while other coastal towns languished or even declined in the later Middle Ages, Poole prospered more than ever. It can hardly have escaped the plague, but it may well have suffered less from raids, for it is tucked well inside its harbour. There was, though, a raid on Poole in 1377, and another in 1405, which was the result of provocation from one Harry Page, or Paye, burgess of Poole, Vice-Admiral of the Cinque Ports, merchant, privateer and pirate. A Spanish source, the Chronicle of Count Don Pedro Nino, related:

> This Arripay came often upon the coast of Castile, and carried away many ships and barks; and he scoured the channel of Flanders so powerfully, that no vessel could pass that way without being taken. This Arripay burnt Gijon and Finisterra, and carried off the crucifix of Finisterra, which was the holiest in all those parts, and much more damage he did in Castile, taking many prisoners, and exacting ransoms.

In 1405, Don Pedro Nino was leading a Franco-Spanish fleet in the Channel when he realised he was near the home town of the infamous Page. He decided to attack it. The French hesitated, but a force of Spaniards landed. They fought with crossbows and, at first, the defenders held them at bay with their more efficient longbows, sheltering behind doors which they took from their hinges. Then Don Pedro led the rest of his Spaniards ashore, shaming the French into following. The Spaniards shouted their national war cry, 'Santiago', no doubt unaware that they shared the same patron saint with Poole. At length, the defenders broke, and fled on the heath. Page was away at the time of the raid, but his brother was killed in the fighting.

7

THE MEDIEVAL CHURCH

The Normans had begun a campaign of church building, and later generations continued it. New churches appeared while older ones were altered, extended and replaced. All the time, the style of building was changing.

The most important break in style was between the Romanesque and the Gothic. Despite many differences, both Saxon and Norman churches are Romanesque, since they have semi-circular arches like those found in Roman buildings. Gothic arches, on the other hand, are pointed. There are three main Gothic styles: Early English, Decorated and Perpendicular. The Early English style developed in the first half of the 13th century and then evolved into the Decorated, which matured soon after 1300. Then came the Black Death in 1348 and building ceased for a time. When it resumed, it was in the Perpendicular style. Because the Decorated style lasted for so short a time, there is little of it to be seen in England, and least of all in Dorset. Here, the only Decorated building of any importance is the unfinished church of Milton Abbey.

The Perpendicular style was born in Gloucester in the 1350s and persisted until the early 17th century. The peak, though, was the 15th century, when the builders achieved as much as the Normans, if not more. Dorset has its share of superb Perpendicular churches. Sherborne Abbey is supreme, but St Peter's, Dorchester, is a fine building, while the towers at Cerne Abbas, Bradford Abbas and Beaminster can bear comparison with the best in Somerset.

During the Middle Ages, church interiors were much more colourful than they are today. Originally, the walls were plastered and covered with paintings, which were not just decorations but picture stories for the benefit of people who could not read. Most of these paintings were destroyed at the time of the Reformation, though some have survived, notably at Tarrant Crawford. Here, there is an Annunciation, along with two series, one telling the legend of St Margaret of Antioch and the other of the Three Quick and the Three Dead. Cranborne has a

Trent church. This is one of Dorset's three medieval spires.

Rood screen, Trent.

St Christopher and a sexist Tree of the Deadly Sins. The tree grows out of a woman's head and is full of arboreal naked girls.

Almost every church had a rood screen separating the chancel from the nave and emphasising the division between the laity and the clergy. The former were confined to their part of the church, the nave, while the priests, shut off in the chancel, interceded with God on their flock's behalf. The Protestant reformers, though, insisted that everyone should have direct access to God and tore down many rood screens. Fortunately, some survived. There is a superb wooden screen at Trent and there are some interesting stone screens, for example at Cerne Abbas and Bradford Abbas.

Three of Dorset's medieval parish churches are outstanding, Wimborne Minster, Whitchurch Canonicorum and Bere Regis.

At Wimborne, Edward the Confessor founded a minster, served by a college of secular canons. The canons had their church and their living quarters, so they formed a community, but, being secular clergy, they worked among the people. Since the Minster was collegiate it needed a choir for its numerous priests, rather than a humble chancel, so the plan is like that of a cathedral, though smaller.

As elsewhere, the Normans pulled down the Saxon church and built a substantial one of their own. During the Middle Ages this was extended in every direction, even downwards with the addition of a crypt. The

58

Crossing tower of Wimborne Minster.

Arcade of Whitchurch Canonicorum church.

result is that all the medieval styles of architecture are represented at Wimborne, even including a little Decorated work.

Legend says that King Alfred's elder brother, Ethelred I of Wessex, is buried in the Minster, where there is a medieval brass to him. The Minster is certainly the resting place of John, Duke of Beaufort, Duke of Lancaster, and his wife Margaret. They were the grandparents of Henry VII and hence the ancestors of our royal family. The couple have a handsome alabaster tomb in the presbytery, both effigies wearing the 'SS' collar of the House of Lancaster; the letters probably stood for 'Spiritus Sanctus'.

As in all great churches there are numerous chapels. In the north transept was the Great Chantry, founded by Thomas de Brembre in 1354. It was endowed in part with crown lands worth £71 and yielding an income of £4 a year. The purpose of a chantry was to pray for the souls of its benefactors, so shortening their time in Purgatory. The money paid the priest who said the masses. Another chantry was founded by Lady Margaret Beaufort, daughter of the couple in the tomb. It was common for a chantry priest to act as schoolmaster and Margaret Beaufort's was required to teach Latin 'to all comers'.

The Minster's relics included part of Christ's manger, some of the ground where He was born, some hairs from His beard, a bone from St Agatha's thigh, one of St Cecilia's joints, one of St Philip's teeth, some of the blood and the hair shirt of St Thomas à Becket and, inevitably, part of the True Cross.

Whitchurch Canonicorum has an imposing Perpendicular tower, one of the best in Dorset, but some Early English work is particularly remarkable, especially in the north arcade. Here, the general shape of the arches, columns and capitals is standard, but the ornament is quite unique, especially the zig-zag round the arch facing the south doorway. Zig-zag is a Norman motif, but not this kind. The most interesting feature of the church, though, is a shrine to its patron saint, St Wite.

The shrine is a plain stone chest, with three openings. Pilgrims came to thrust their diseased limbs into these openings, hoping for a cure, or, if the sick could not come themselves, others would put handkerchiefs or garments through the holes and take them to heal their owners. Above the shrine is a stone coffin. In 1900 the church wall cracked, damaging the shrine, and the coffin was opened so that it could be repaired. Inside was a lead casket with a Latin inscription reading, 'Here lie the remains of St Wite.' The casket itself contained some bones, which might or might not have belonged to a woman.

Nothing certain is known about St Wite. According to local tradition, she was a Saxon who was killed by the Danes. There is also a story that she escaped from pirates, but only at the cost of two fingers cut off with an axe; she then walked on the water to Brittany. There are some carved panels on the tower, one of which shows an axe and another a ship and an axe.

Bere Regis was the birthplace of John Morton (1423–1500). He became rector of Bloxworth and later, Archbishop of Canterbury, a Cardinal and Lord Chancellor to Henry VII. The king believed in remaining solvent and he found a willing helper in Morton, who is credited with the famous 'fork'. It had two prongs. A man who was extravagant was told it was obvious he could afford high taxes. A man who was careful with his money was told that he must have large savings, so he, too, had to pay. Probably 'Morton's fork' was a joke, but Morton did visit nobles to assess them for tax.

St John the Baptist's at Bere Regis is a fine church, full of interest, but its chief glory is its marvellous roof, almost certainly the gift of John Morton. This roof is remarkable for its elaborate ornament, especially the figures of the twelve apostles, all in 15th century costume. St Peter is there with his keys, as is St James, the pilgrim, with his staff and cockle shell, and Judas, clutching his bag of money. A particularly ugly boss is said to represent the face of Cardinal Morton.

At the time of the Normans, Dorset's religious houses were all Benedictine. That meant they followed the rule drawn up by St Benedict when he founded the order in the 6th century. The rule was none too strict, but even so it was interpreted loosely and as the monasteries grew rich, so the temptation to enjoy an easy life increased. It was clear that the Benedictines were failing in their duty, so in 1098 an abbey was founded at Cîteaux in Burgundy whose rule required asceticism, simplicity and isolation from the world. This was the beginning of the Cistercian order.

The Cistercians owed much to the third abbot of their mother house, an Englishman called Stephen Harding. He might have been born in Sherborne, and was certainly educated in the abbey. It was Harding who, in 1119, drafted his Order's constitution, the Carta Caritatis, and it was he who gave the movement the impetus that carried it over much of Christian Europe. Its first monastery in England was founded at Waverley, Surrey, in 1128.

There were three Cistercian houses in Dorset, the monasteries of Forde and Bindon and the nunnery of Tarrant Crawford. None of them adhered too strictly to the ideals of their order.

In 1136 Sir Richard de Brioniis founded a monastery at Brightley in Devon and twelve monks left Waverley to people it. The site seemed ideal for Cistercians, for it was remote and infertile, but instead of

Roof of Bere Regis church. The boss said to represent Cardinal Morton is the first one, in the centre.

leading a hard life as their order required, the monks decided to return to Waverley. On their way back they were met by Adelicia, sister of Sir Richard de Brioniis, who offered them the manor of Thorncombe and a plum site by the river Axe. They accepted, and began the building of Forde Abbey.

Bindon's story is similar. At first it was at Little Bindon, near Lulworth Cove, but that was too remote for the monks who moved to a site near Wool.

The nunnery at Tarrant Crawford was founded by Richard Poore, the famous Bishop of Salisbury who built the town's marvellous cathedral. He was born at Tarrant Crawford. Evidence on the ground tells us something of the story of his nunnery. It was built in chalk country where, characteristically, all the Dorset Tarrants are strung along the valley of the stream that bears this name. The one exception was the medieval village of Tarrant Crawford, the remains of which are in a dry valley half a mile to the south-east of the nunnery and the modern hamlet. Almost certainly, the village once occupied the place that was taken by the nunnery. The two could not exist side by side, however, because Cistercians had to have solitude. Consequently, the villagers were ordered away from their water and their meadows and given an inhospitable site which, eventually, they abandoned. This conduct was typical of Cistercians, but one wonders what moved Bishop Poore to treat his native village so badly.

Attached to the nunnery, though living in complete seclusion, were three anchoresses. Poore may have been the author of *The Ancren Riwle*, a code of conduct for such women:

> Next to your flesh, ye shall wear no flaxen cloth, except it be of hards and of coarse canvas.
>
> Wear no iron nor haircloth, nor hedgehog skins, and do not beat yourselves therewith, nor with a scourge of leather nor leaded. And do not with holly nor with briars cause yourselves to bleed without leave of your confessor. And do not, at one time, use too many flagellations. Let your shoes be thick and warm. In summer ye are at liberty to go and sit barefoot.
>
> My dear sisters, love your windows as little as possible. See that they be small. Let the cloth upon them be twofold. Black cloth does less harm to the eyes, is thicker against the wind, more difficult to see through, and keeps its colour better . . .
>
> Let no man see them unveiled, nor without a hood. Let them look low. They ought not to kiss nor lovingly embrace any man, neither

of their acquaintance, nor a stranger, nor to romp nor frolic with him . . .

Ye shall not possess any beast, my dear sisters, except only a cat.

Today, little remains of the Tarrant Crawford nunnery, but somewhere among the farm buildings and fields are the graves of Bishop Poore and of Joan, wife of Alexander II of Scotland and sister of Henry III of England.

The religious houses were rich. Cerne Abbey was by no means the wealthiest, but at the time of the Domesday survey it held 17 manors in Dorset with a combined population of about 1,500 people, 100 ploughlands and, curiously, five and a half mills. That was only the beginning, since Cerne and the other houses went on accumulating endowments through the Middle Ages. In 1122, for example, Bishop Roger of Salisbury presented Sherborne Abbey with nine manors and the priories of Horton in Dorset and Kidwelly in South Wales.

Pilgrims were a good source of income, and they were attracted by relics. Christchurch had the sandals and cowl of Thomas à Becket, a piece of wood from Christ's cradle (a welcome change from His cross) and a stone from His sepulchre. Sherborne already held the remains of St Wulfsin and later it acquired those of St Juthware. This innocent girl was beheaded on the orders of her wicked stepmother, but before expiring she walked to Halstock church where she placed her severed head on the altar.

The wealthiest religious house in Dorset must have been the nunnery at Shaftesbury, with its cult of the royal martyr, St Edward. A seventeenth century cleric, Thomas Fuller, wrote that if the abbess of Shaftesbury had married the abbot of Glastonbury, their heir would have owned more property than the king of England.

As we have seen, the Normans made a clean sweep of the Saxon monasteries and then, over the centuries, the Norman monasteries themselves were altered. Most of the work, and the best of it, was done in the 15th century. Monastery churches have survived at Christchurch, Milton Abbas and Sherborne, and each has its own story.

The crossing tower at Christchurch fell some time early in the 13th century, and the monks did not replace it. During the 15th century, a tower was built at the west end and a lady chapel at the east end, while the chancel was replaced with a magnificent choir. Inside, all is harmony, but outside the building looks disjointed. It is known locally as 'the train'. It is unfortunate that the room over the lady chapel rises above the choir as it is better, aesthetically, for the end of a building to be lower than its adjoining parts. Even more painful is the way the choir aisles block

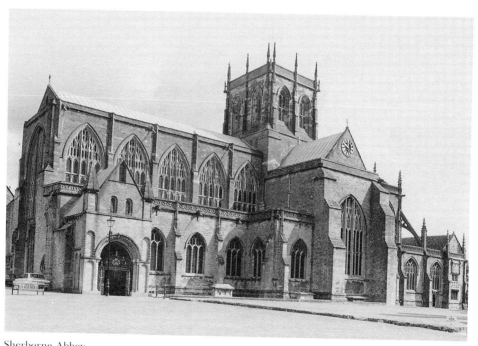

Sherborne Abbey.

half a window on each side of the lady chapel. This cannot have been planned. One theory is that the lady chapel was built first, separate from the rest of the church. The builders then demolished the Norman east end and cobbled the new choir to the lady chapel as best they could.

The church of Milton Abbey was struck by lightning in 1309. 'Totaliter inflammavit', lamented the chronicler. The monks started rebuilding using the style then in fashion, which was Decorated. By 1348 they had reached the crossing, where they finished the south transept and started the tower. Then the Black Death struck and work ceased. Late in the 15th century, the north transept and the tower were finished, but that was all. A blank wall now blocks the west arch of the crossing.

It is likely that at Sherborne the Normans left a good deal of Saxon work intact. In the 13th century a lady chapel was added at the east end and Bishop Roger's chapel on the north side, both in the Early English style. The result must have been a hotch-potch. Then, early in the 15th century, Abbot John Brunyng began a series of works that were to transform the church into what is still the finest building in Dorset. The choir was new and, though the other parts remained, they were for the most part given Perpendicular cladding. Huge windows replaced the smaller openings of the earlier styles. The result was a building which is spacious, light and, superficially at least, uniform in style.

Fan vaulting in choir of Sherborne Abbey.

During the rebuilding at Sherborne, a trivial dispute flared up, literally as well as metaphorically, into a major row. The parish church of the town, All Hallows, stood against the west wall of the abbey church. A door connected the two which the townsfolk used for processions and, since they were allowed no font of their own, for christenings. In 1437 the monks narrowed this doorway, whereupon the townsfolk retaliated by ringing their bells when the monks wanted to sleep and by setting up a font in All Hallows. The abbot sent a butcher to demolish the font. Due to the rebuilding, part of the abbey church was then covered with a temporary roof of thatch. A priest of All Hallows shot a flaming arrow into this thatch, starting a blaze that destroyed the roof, melted the lead and bells and marked the stonework. The piers are red in places to this day.

Both the choir and the nave at Sherborne have fan vaults which are not only magnificent but interesting. Most books on church architecture explain that in the later Middle Ages, master masons wanted their buildings to be light, so they pierced the walls with large windows. As a result, the walls were so weakened that they could not support the roof, still less a stone vault. The answer was to make a complicated skeleton of powerful buttresses, in which the walls were little more than screens. The roof and vault of a choir or nave needed flying buttresses, which transferred their weight to the buttresses that stood against the walls of the aisles. At Sherborne, the choir does indeed have flying buttresses, but the nave, in defiance of all the theories, has none. Moreover, in the 19th century it was the choir vault which came close to collapse, while the nave vault stood firm, and still does.

Abbots of the late Middle Ages treated themselves magnificently. One of the fragments remaining at Cerne is the splendid porch to the abbot's lodging. In Pevsner's words, the abbot's hall at Milton Abbey 'speaks of wealth, pride and heady display.' Neither, though, is as sumptuous as the hall and entrance porch which Abbot Chard built for himself at Forde. Chard's work was finished just in time for the dissolution of the monasteries in 1539.

As we have seen, a rich person could shorten his or her time in Purgatory by endowing a chantry. Humble folk had to combine to form a religious guild, like that of St George in Poole. Its main purpose was to say masses for the souls of dead members, so it had an altar in St James's church, where it kept a light always burning. The guild also gave its members a degree of security in this life, for it maintained some almshouses for those who had 'decayed' and it distributed charity to the widows and orphans of those who had died.

8

NEW RELIGIONS FOR OLD

In the sixteenth century much of Western Europe went through a crisis known as the Reformation. Individuals, communities and entire states rejected the Roman Catholic religion to become Protestant. The two most important leaders of the Reformation were Martin Luther, a monk from Saxony, and John Calvin a French lawyer and classical scholar who moved to Geneva. Much of the debate was about theological questions, mainly concerned with the saving of souls, but other issues involved this world rather than the next.

Christ had given St Peter two swords, one representing the spiritual power of the Church and the other the temporal power of the State. The two authorities co-existed, uneasily, through the Middle Ages, but where the Reformation took hold, this duality came to an end. The countries of north Germany became Lutheran and the state dominated the church. In Calvin's Geneva, on the other hand, the church dominated the state. Luther, it has been said, created a state church, while Calvin created a church state.

In England, Henry VIII chose what seemed to him the best of all worlds, making himself Supreme Head of the church as the Lutheran princes had done, but keeping the rest of the Catholic faith intact. During the minority of his son, Edward VI, a group of Calvinist nobles held power and then his daughter Mary returned the country to Rome. Finally, Elizabeth founded the Church of England, which was moderately Protestant, with herself as Supreme Governor.

After Henry VIII broke with Rome he dissolved the monasteries. It has been said that religious houses owned a third of the land in England and that their income was nearly double that of the Crown. Henry seized their treasures, buildings and land and sold them, so bringing about the largest transfer of property in England since the Norman Conquest.

Dorset's religious houses were dissolved in 1539. Any monk or nun who resisted risked a horrible death, but in Dorset none did. The abbot of Cerne was accused of cohabiting with women, rape, spending abbey funds on his bastards and allowing his monks to play cards all

Great Barn, Abbotsbury. The barn, now only partly roofed, is 272 feet long, making it one of the largest in England. On the hill, is St Catherine's Chapel, a marker for shipping, as well as a place of worship. Below the chapel, are some strip lynchets.

night and attend mass without washing, but that was only to win public approval for the closing of his monastery. So far from being punished, he was given a generous pension of £100 a year. One of his monks, Thomas Lillington, became vicar of Affpuddle, where he carved a pulpit and some handsome bench ends. At Sherborne, Abbot John Barnstable received a pension of £100 and the living of Stalbridge. Prior John Dunster had a pension of £12 and the vicarage of Osborne. William Vowell, an ordinary monk, had a pension of 13 marks, or £6 13s 4d.

Most of the profits of the dissolution of the monasteries came from the sale of their lands. The Dorset gentry were eager to buy. Woodbury Hill at Bere Regis, for example, had been shared between Tarrant nunnery and the Turbervilles, but at the dissolution, the Turbervilles took it all. This transaction is remarkable because the Turbervilles were Catholics, and saw no reason to change their faith. Other Catholic families also bought monastery lands.

The monastery buildings had a chequered fate. The churches at Milton Abbas, Sherborne and Christchurch are still intact because in all three places the townsfolk bought them. The people of Sherborne paid £66 13s 4d for the building and £247 17s 6d for the roof lead and bells. Apart from the three churches, all else is fragments and ruins. At one time nothing could be seen of Shaftesbury Abbey, but some of the foundations have now been uncovered. Milton Abbey's hall is part of an 18th century house. The Strangways, who bought Abbotsbury, used much of the stone to build a manor house, but there are some ruins, as well as an impressive tithe barn. The gatehouse of Cerne is part of Abbey Farm, while the porch to the abbot's lodging stands in isolation, as does a building that may have been the guest house. The tithe barn, part of which is now a private dwelling, is in another part of the village. At Forde, the church and half the cloisters were lost, but in 1649 what remained was bought by Cromwell's Attorney General, Edmund Prideaux. He employed Inigo Jones to convert the buildings into a sumptuous house, preserving the magnificent work of Thomas Chard, the last abbot.

In the reign of Edward VI, the young king's Protector, the Duke of Somerset, dissolved the chantries and the religious guilds. That meant the end, for example, of Lady Margaret Beaufort's chantry at Wimborne and St George's Guild at Poole. Such guilds and charities offered prayers for the souls of the dead, hoping to shorten their time in Purgatory. Somerset had the excuse he needed to seize their wealth because Protestants did not believe in Purgatory. Neither did extreme Protestants approve of anything in churches that suggested idolatry, so

Forde Abbey. Abbot Chard's entrance tower and hall are to the left of the central block. The north range of the cloisters is to the right. The wing jutting forward on the right was the chapter house. The central block itself is Prideaux's saloon, above an eighteenth century loggia. The bays to the left of the hall are also Prideaux's work.

the government ordered the destruction of wall paintings, rood screens and statues of Christ and the saints. Not every parish obeyed these orders to the letter so that samples of medieval craftsmanship survive, like the rood screen at Trent.

During the religious changes, most people had little to fear as long as they kept their convictions to themselves. Cardinal Reginald Pole, though, attacked Henry VIII's claim to be Supreme Head of the Church. He was safely abroad, but Henry imprisoned his mother, Margaret Countess of Salisbury, for two years and then ordered her execution. As she refused to put her head on the block, she was killed standing. She had prepared a beautiful chantry for herself in Christchurch priory, but was buried in the traitors' cemetery in the Tower of London. The chantry still stands, though the Salisbury arms were torn from its walls.

Under Edward VI, Poole's rector, Thomas Hancock, preached the Protestant faith so vigorously that he provoked a riot in St James's church. The Catholics, he said, 'did call me knave and my wife strumpet, some of them threatening me that they would make me draw my guts after me.' When Mary came to the throne and brought England back to Catholicism, Hancock took the optimistic view that she only wished to exercise her religion in peace, so he continued to 'put down the glorious gospel of Jesus Christ' and to denounce the Catholics' 'idolatrous desire to have their superstitious ceremony and their idolish mass.' Soon disillusioned about Queen Mary's intentions, he fled abroad.

The story of handsome John Russell of Weymouth is quite different. His brilliant career began because he could speak Spanish. In 1506 the ship carrying Queen Joanna of Castile and her husband the Archduke Philip was driven ashore at Weymouth. The governor of the town, Sir Thomas Trenchard, had the royal pair brought to his home, Wolveton House, and, needing an interpreter, sent for John Russell. Russell then went to Windsor with the Queen and Archduke, where he so impressed Henry VII that he was made a gentleman of the privy chamber. Russell blossomed under Henry VIII, fighting in France, acting as ambassador to Pope Clement VII and helping with the grisly execution of the abbot of Glastonbury. Under Edward VI, there was a rebellion in the west against Somerset's religious changes. Russell suppressed it with the aid of German and Italian mercenaries, for which service he was made Earl of Bedford. At the same time as acting as the extreme Protestants' strong right arm, Russell was keeping on good terms with that devout Catholic, Princess Mary. She rewarded him with office when she became Queen, even sending him to Spain to arrange her marriage with Philip II. Elizabeth's accession in 1558 would have been the final test of Russell's agility, but he had died in 1555.

Queen Elizabeth founded the Church of England, which was moderately Protestant, a compromise that satisfied most of her subjects, though not the more zealous Catholics. There were plots to put Mary, Queen of Scots on the throne; Jesuit priests, the shock troops of the Counter Reformation, arrived to win back people to Rome; Philip II sent the Armada to conquer the country. As the threat grew, so the measures against Catholics became more severe, priests being the main targets. About 140 Catholics were executed, 98 of them missionary priests.

Several Catholics were executed in Dorchester. They are known as the 'Chideock Martyrs' because of their links with one of Dorset's leading Catholic families, the Arundels of Chideock. In law the priests were guilty of high treason, so they were hanged, drawn and quartered, the first to suffer being Thomas Pilchard in 1587. The last of the Catholics to die was another priest, Hugh Green, in 1642. The people of Dorchester dismembered his body and kicked his head round the town.

During the Middle Ages the Church and the religious guilds were supposed, in theory, to care for the poor. After the Reformation, others took up the burden. At Poole, the Guild of St George was dissolved under Edward VI, and all its property confiscated, but the town at once took over the Guild's almshouses and bought back their endowments from the Crown. Wealthy individuals also helped by endowing charities. An endowment was almost always a gift of land or property, which was meant to ensure that the charity would last 'for ever', as was often the wish. The rents paid for whatever the donor decreed. It could range from a dole of bread at Christmas, to a set of almshouses with pensions for the inmates.

Blandford had what was called the 'Church Almshouses'. It is not known when they were founded, but the town had taken responsibility for them by the 16th century. There are signs of Puritan influence in the early 17th century, for the accounts show a payment of £1 a year to a clergyman for reading prayers, and there was a rule book. Inmates could not take in their children or lodgers, they were not allowed to marry or fornicate and they had to obey their steward and the constable.

Whether a town or village was well endowed with charities or not depended on chance. Wimborne St Giles, for example, acquired a fine set of almshouses only because Sir Anthony Ashley recovered from an illness and wanted to show his gratitude. But, as we shall see, changes in agriculture brought an increase in poverty, so during Elizabeth's reign Parliament made a series of laws which were consolidated in the Poor Law Act of 1601. The basic principle was that each parish should be responsible for its own poor. Those who owned or rented property were

Master's house, Sherborne Abbey. The coat of arms is that of Edward VI.

assessed for a poor rate. The 'able-bodied' were found work, the parish providing tools and materials, and paying the wages. The 'impotent poor', such as orphans, the sick and the elderly were given food, clothing and shelter. The men who levied the rate and gave the relief were chosen by the local JPs and known as 'overseers of the poor'. They were ordinary villagers, and being ratepayers themselves they were not often generous to the poor. To deter people from going 'on the parish', they humiliated those who did.

Education, like the care of the poor, was the duty of the Church during the Middle Ages, and schools suffered, at first, under the Reformation. Some survived, with difficulty, while others closed. Towns, though, needed schools, and both Edward VI and Elizabeth encouraged them, for they wanted their young men to be loyal Protestants, especially those training for the Ministry.

Wimborne's school closed, briefly, but the inhabitants revived it and kept it going until a charter of 1563 granted them a new grammar school. It was known as Queen Elizabeth's School. Dorchester's grammar school was a new foundation in 1567. It was called Hardye's School after Thomas Hardye of Frampton, who endowed it. It was destroyed in Dorchester's great fire of 1613, but the headmaster, the Rev Robert Cheeke, rebuilt it, largely at his own expense. King's School, Sherborne, was granted a royal licence in 1552. As the name suggests, Edward VI had the credit for founding it, but it may have been a re-foundation. It was housed in the monastery buildings, where it still is, while the lady chapel of the abbey church was converted to a residence for the headmaster. The partitions were so thin that a 19th century vicar complained, 'The master's lady hears all our chants, and we hear all their polkas.'

ELIZABETHAN AND JACOBEAN DORSET

In the early 16th century many Dorset farmers were still growing food mainly for themselves and their families, with only small surpluses for sale. As time went on, though, they found incentives to produce more.

The local market expanded. Assuming Dorset kept pace with the rest of England, its population nearly doubled between 1500 and 1700. We cannot be sure of that, but we do know that there were 21 market towns in the county and they were not all self-sufficient, even though they had their own fields. The London market also increased in importance. The city's population may have been 50,000 in 1500, 200,000 in 1600 and 400,000 in 1700. A third market was the woollen industry, which is described in the next chapter. To supply the new markets, Dorset farmers kept more cattle and sheep.

The cattle were reared in the north and west of the county. Milk could not be sent to London, while Dorset has never been famous for its cheese, but the area between Lyme Regis and Bridport became noted for its butter. This was salted and packed in tubs so that it could stand an uncomfortable journey by waggon or ship. The skimmed milk was made into an inferior cheese which was sold locally. Cattle were driven to Essex where graziers fattened them before taking them to Smithfield.

Sheep were reared on the chalk. They were more important than cattle. In 1633 Thomas Gerard wrote that the downs were 'all overspread with innumerable Flockes of Sheepe' and in 1659 Edward Leigh claimed, though probably with some exaggeration, that there were 300,000 sheep within six miles of Dorchester. Many of the sheep went to Buckinghamshire and Hertfordshire where they were fattened for London.

Those Dorset farmers who increased their output did so by reclaiming land and by adopting new techniques.

In the vale, people continued nibbling at the woodland, making small, irregular fields. On the downs, more and more large, rectangular enclosures appeared. The more fertile parts of the heath were also

75

attacked. Early in the 17th century, John Avery of Uddens House and John Bankes of Corfe Castle each reclaimed about 400 acres of heath. Between 1630 and 1646, Sir John Horsey and other 'adventurers' tried to drain the Fleet, but failed because they had set themselves the impossible task of making Chesil Bank watertight. 'By reason of Stormy windes and tempests the Sea did force or cast upp much Sea Water over and through the gravelly or sandy bank.'

One of the new techniques was the folding of sheep. At night, the shepherd confined his flock to a part of the field, using hurdles. The next night he moved his hurdles, and so on, until he had covered the whole field. The sheep dunged the ground evenly and when it was ploughed, it gave a good crop of cereals. The farmer not only had as much mutton and wool as before, but the corn as well.

Under the medieval system of farming, arable and grassland did not change, but this is not good practice. When grassland becomes tired, it is best to plough it, crop it for a few years, and then seed it anew. When arable is exhausted, it helps to convert it to grass for a time. Some farmers realised this as early as the 16th century and began to plough up and grass down their fields alternately, a technique they called 'up and down husbandry'. Land no longer lay fallow, but even so its fertility improved dramatically. Blith, a 17th century author, wrote, 'One acre beareth the fruit of three, and two acres are preserved to graze.'

Another improvement was the floating of water meadows, which was an Italian idea that came to England in the 17th century. Grass likes an abundance of moisture and if it is well watered at appropriate times, its growing season is much longer. The simplest way was to dam a stream and let it flood the land, but the catchwork method was much better. This meant digging a channel along the top of the field and allowing the water to spill over the edge, so that it ran, about an inch deep, down the entire field. If the stream had run through a farmyard or, what was much the same thing, a town or village, then it was rich in nutrients. If, as was usual in Dorset, it had come from chalk, then it was calcareous.

The watering began at Christmas, to be repeated at intervals until, by mid-March, there was already a good crop of grass. Ewes and lambs were put to graze until early May. There was more watering until the middle of July, when the meadows gave excellent crops of hay. Yet more watering followed and by September there was enough grass to support dairy cattle until Christmas.

Once, a shortage of winter feed had meant slaughtering many animals in the autumn, but water meadows gave massive crops of hay, as well as good grazing early and late in the year. The earliest reference to water meadows in Dorset is 1629 when, after much debate, the farmers of

Puddletown decided to make them. Moreton, Bovington and Winfrith Newburgh were all floating their meadows later in the century.

Farming improvements usually went hand in hand with enclosure. The open field system was flexible enough, but for some changes everyone had to agree. For example, an obstinate minority could have prevented the floating of water meadows at Puddletown. Generally speaking, it was better for a progressive farmer if he could disentangle his own land from that of his neighbours.

Land reclaimed from the forests, downs and heaths was at once enclosed. But there was enclosure, too, on land that was already being farmed. The common pasture could be divided easily enough, though the arable was more complicated because the holdings were of small, scattered strips. Over the years, tenants might consolidate their strips by exchange, purchase or marriage and once a man held a sizeable block of strips, he might put a hedge round it. For example, at Gillingham in about 1650, one Barnes made an enclosure in the middle of Magstone Field. Thus, the common arable dwindled slowly over the centuries.

These changes did not take place everywhere in Dorset by any means. While some farmers were enclosing land, floating water meadows and folding sheep, the people of Ashmore, for example, went on cultivating their common fields just as their ancestors had done since Saxon times.

There has been much debate about enclosures. In Sir Thomas More's *Utopia* there is a famous passage describing how sheep were eating men. Tyrannical landlords were enclosing their farms and turning their arable to pasture, so that they could keep sheep. They then needed far fewer workers, so they evicted the unwanted people, who became wandering beggars. At the end of the 16th century, the Rev Thomas Bastard of Bere Regis expressed similar ideas. In his *Epigrams* he wrote of a thief he claimed to know:

> Howses by three, and seaven and ten he raseth,
> To make the common gleabe his private land;
> Our country Cities cruell he defaceth,
> And grass grows greene where litle Troy did stand,
> The forlorne father hanging downe his head,
> His outcast company drawne up and downe,
> The pining labourer doth begge his bread,
> The plowswayne seeks his dinner from the towne.
> Sheep hauve eate up our medows and our downes,
> Our corne, our wood, whole villages and townes.

There is other evidence of oppression. In the early 16th century the people of Bincombe and Winterborne Came went to the Court of Star Chamber to prevent their landlord, Sir William Fyloll, from enclosing the common fields. We do not know if they were successful. Early in the 17th century the royal forest of Gillingham was disafforested and much of the land was then enclosed. The local people lost their common rights and there were riots in 1624 and from 1642 to 1645. When John Uddens enclosed 400 acres of heath the poor complained that they could no longer cut turf for fuel. But how much enclosure was there and how much of it was forced on unwilling tenants?

At Iwerne Minster in 1546 the tenants agreed with their lord to consolidate their holdings and enclose them, but they left 80 acres of common pasture untouched. In 1577 the tenants at Charminster fell out with their lord, William Harlyn, because he wanted to enclose part of the common fields. In the end, Harlyn and those who wished to enclose did so, leaving the rest to go on as before. Half the common fields of Hinton St Mary had been enclosed by 1600, though nearly all the tenants still held land on what remained of the open fields. At West Parley, the owners of the heath disagreed over its enclosure and went to the Court of Chancery. The court made an award that was scrupulously fair. As the heath varied in quality, each man was given a strip that ran the width of it. John Bolton's was two miles long and 22 yards wide.

It is almost certain, then, that there was no enclosure of entire villages. Further it would seem that enclosure was sometimes by agreement, and even where it was enforced, there were attempts to safeguard the rights of everyone concerned. Moreover, enclosures were not the main reason for hardship. The woollen industry was in depression from time to time, for example in the 1620s. There were epidemics of smallpox, while the plague returned on occasion. It struck Mapperton in 1582. The dead from that village had always been buried in Netherbury, but when the Mapperton mourners arrived with their plague victims, the people of Netherbury drove them away. The Mapperton folk had to retreat to South Warren Hill, where they buried their dead in a mass grave and planted conifers to prevent it being disturbed. The survivors put bunches of flowers under a tree, which became known as the 'posy tree'.

Other evidence is more cheerful. Dorset has a fair number of substantial farmhouses that date from this period, such as Sturt Farm at Stalbridge and Manor Farm at Trent. They show that some relatively humble people, at least, were enjoying comfortable lives.

Under the Tudors and Stuarts, the Dorset gentry gained many new recruits. Some promoted themselves from the yeomanry. The Strodes of

Manor Farm, Trent

Parnham, for example, gradually accumulated wealth and then, in 1522, Robert Strode married Elizabeth, granddaughter of Sir William Hardy, Henry VII's Chief Baron of the Exchequer. To see what that marriage meant for the Strode family it is only necessary to visit Parnham House.

Merchants became landed gentry. John Henning of Poole built a substantial, but very conventional manor house at Poxwell. Humphrey Weld from London bought Lulworth Castle. It had been started by the second and third Viscounts Bindon, and Weld finished it. Far from conventional, it is a work of fantasy, like Henry VIII's Nonsuch Palace.

Royal servants bought landed estates. A Cornish lawyer called John Tregonwell was one of the proctors involved with Henry VIII's divorce. He was knighted for his services, and at the dissolution of the monasteries he bought Milton Abbey, which he turned into a home. Robert Seymer, who was Teller of the Exchequer late in Elizabeth's reign bought Stoke Lake and built Hanford House. Sir John Bankes, Charles I's Attorney General bought Corfe Castle in 1635 and became one of Dorset's improving landlords.

For a time, the Dorset gentry included Sir Walter Raleigh, one of Queen Elizabeth's 'favourites'. One day, when travelling through Sherborne, he passed the castle, then the property of the Bishop of Salisbury. As soon as Raleigh saw the castle, he coveted it. His horse fell the moment he had the evil thought, but he decided to persuade the Queen to obtain the castle for him. He knew love alone would not be enough, so he gave her a jewel worth £250 as a bribe to 'make the bishop'. Elizabeth induced the bishop to lease the castle to the Crown and she then leased it to Raleigh. That was in 1592. What Elizabeth did not know was that in 1591 Raleigh had secretly married one of her ladies in waiting, Bess Throckmorton. When Elizabeth found out, she sent Raleigh and his wife to the Tower, in separate quarters. She released them after five weeks but banished them from Court, so that Raleigh spent more time at Sherborne than he had expected. Lady Raleigh found her husband's dream castle most inconvenient, so they built a lodge nearby and just used the castle for such things as banquets and pageants.

While in Dorset, Raleigh kept what some considered strange company, including the mathematician Thomas Hariot and the scientist and explorer Adrian Gilbert. Raleigh also expressed unorthodox views and after he had been indiscreet during a dinner party at Wolveton House, the Privy Council ordered an enquiry into 'Sir Walter Raleigh's School of Atheism'. Atheism in those days meant holding outlandish opinions, rather than a disbelief in God. The inquiry took place at Cerne Abbas in 1593. Raleigh was acquitted, even though the Commission included his enemy, the spiteful Lord Thomas Howard of Bindon.

Dorset has many attractive country houses of the 16th and 17th centuries. This was the time of the Renaissance when European builders revived the architecture of Greece and Rome. The movement, which began in Italy, spread slowly in England. Before 1700 it went through four stages: Tudor, Elizabethan, Jacobean and Late Stuart.

Sandford Orcas manor house, of about 1530, is a good Tudor building. Some detail in the porch shows that the owner may at least have heard of classical columns, but that apart, the house looks much the same as many of the late Middle Ages. The shape is irregular, there are large, mullioned windows, high pitched roofs and pointed gables with finials. The hall, though, is unlike any of the Middle Ages. Instead of being two storeys high and open to a roof with elaborate beams, it is only one storey high and has a plaster ceiling.

By Elizabethan times, classical details such as columns and semi-circular arches were becoming fairly usual. For example, the owner of Hamoon Manor added a Renaissance porch to his thatched house. A more important advance was making houses symmetrical, for symmetry is one of the most important features of classical buildings. The usual plan, though, was anything but classical, being E-shaped. The middle stroke of the E was an elaborate porch, while the long strokes were

Porch of Sandford Orcas Manor House

Sandford Orcas Manor House

Kingston Lacy

wings, turned at right angles, to give extra rooms without making the front ridiculously long.

Though it was built in the early 17th century, the east front of Parnham House is Elizabethan in style. The plan is E-shaped and there is at least an attempt at symmetry. Everything else though, is traditional. There are large mullioned windows, some of them bays and some oriels; there is a steep pitched roof, with pointed gables and finials; the chimneys are prominent, for a fireplace was still a status symbol.

Sherborne New Castle, which is mainly Jacobean, marks another step forward. The central block was built by Raleigh. It is fairly modest, but in 1617 James I gave it to Sir John Digby, who flanked it with two long wings, so that the plan became H-shaped. Digby also added classical entrances to the courtyards and to the house. The windows no longer dominate the façade, having only single mullions. The low pitched roofs are hidden behind balustrades. There are no pointed gables and finials.

Kingston Lacy was built by Sir Ralph Bankes after the Civil War, to replace Corfe Castle, which the Roundheads had damaged beyond repair. The architect was Sir Roger Pratt. All the traditional features have now vanished and only the overhanging eaves distinguish this style from the purely classical. Kingston Lacy was a superb Late Stuart house until about 1840, when it was mauled by the designer of the Houses of Parliament, Charles Barry. To visualise the house as it was, we must imagine away the spindly chimneys on the corners and add a half storey which Barry concealed, so destroying Pratt's excellent proportions.

10

THE TOWNS AND INDUSTRY

Dorset's towns attracted many compliments. For example, in 1613 Dorchester was described as, 'beautified with many stately buildings and fair streets, flourishing full of all sorts of tradesmen and artificers, plenty with abundance revealed in her bosom, with a wise and civil government.'

We can gain some idea of what the towns were like, because there are buildings from this period still standing. Sherborne has several, notably Abbeylands in Cheap Street. The house is half timbered, with the upper storey overhanging, there are mullioned windows and the roofs are steeply pitched, with high pointed gables. All this is traditional, but as a

Sixteenth century shops at Sherborne

concession to the Renaissance there is a vaguely classical porch. In Half Moon Street there is something rarely found in England, a complete row of 16th century shops. The shop fronts are modern, but the first floor is intact.

Old Weymouth keeps its original plan, with narrow, winding streets. In Trinity Street, the Old Rooms Inn and Nos 2–3 date from the 17th century. Once again there are mullioned windows, steep pitched roofs and high pointed gables, but both buildings are symmetrical, which shows Renaissance influence.

Poole took a census in 1574, which gave a count of 1,375, but this is a rare statistic indeed. The only certain fact about the towns' populations in general is that they were small. Dorchester and Wareham still had space inside their ancient fortifications, while estimates for Weymouth and Melcombe Regis in the late 16th century give anything between 665 and 2,000.

Even though the towns were picturesque and small, they had problems. There were endemic diseases and the plague returned again and again. Poole's accounts give some idea of a visitation in 1645:

> For pitch and tar for the sick people to burn in their houses – 4s 9d
> Paid William Young for a load of turfs and for his horse to draw dead corpses – 6s 0d
> The charge of building of 4 pest houses – £22 13s 6d
> For digging of graves to the gunner and Andrew's boy – 2s 0d
> For pots and pills – 2s 5d
> For the box of drugs had from Salisbury – £3
> For a shroud for Widow Milledge – 4s 1d

Other towns helped. Christchurch sent £9 13s 7d and '6 bushels of Hampshire corn which made but 5 bushels Poole measure.' Southampton gave £50 6s 7d and Portsmouth £23. Cheselbourne provided 18 sheepskins, though what use they were is not clear. The Isle of Wight donated 80 cheeses, seven barrels of butter and 16 quarters of wheat. It was not entirely philanthropy that inspired these gifts. When a town had the plague, its authorities usually forbade the inhabitants to leave, and it was in everyone's interest to help enforce the quarantine. Anthony Ashley Cooper said of Poole in 1645, 'Plague and famine busily contend for eminence, and the distressed inhabitants, impatient of either of their reign, threaten to break out to the inevitable danger and ruin of the places adjacent.'

Like London, many places had their great fires, and some had several, the main reasons being thatched roofs and carelessness. There was a huge fire at Dorchester in 1613. According to one account, the town lost 170 houses worth £40,000, while another account gives 300 houses worth £200,000. The town became a 'heap of ashes for travellers that pass by to sigh at.' In 1623, 35 houses were burnt and there were still more conflagrations in 1687 and 1697. Much of Bere Regis was destroyed in 1633. Brawling soldiers burnt Beaminster during the Civil War and the town was lost again in 1684.

People took what precautions they could. In the porch of Bere Regis church there are hooks for pulling burning thatch from houses. When anyone was made a freeman of Poole it was usual for him to give the town a large leather bucket. In 1629 the corporation of Dorchester tried to remove the 'danger of maulting and dying houses' by appointing inspectors 'to will and require all those persons that have dangerous howses to repaire and amend it or else to desist from maulting or dying untill the same shall be repaired or amended.'

Water was a daily problem for many townsfolk, the people of Shaftesbury being especially unfortunate since they had to go to Enmore Green, which was not only at the very foot of their hill but outside the town boundary. Each year they performed a ceremony which must surely have pagan origins. The town records of 1527 describe it:

> Hit is the custome time out of remembrance, that the Soundhey nexte after Holy Roode day in May, every yeare, every parish within the borough of Shaston shall come down into Enmore Green, with their mynstralls and myrth of game; and from one of the clocke till too of the clocke, by the space of one hole hower, theire shall they daunce; and the meyer of Shaston shall see the quene's bayliffe have a penny loffe, a gallon of ale, and a calve's head, with a payer of gloves; and if the daunce fayle that day and that the quene's bayliffe have not his duty, then the said bayliffe shall stop the water of the wells of Enmore from the borough of Shaston.

As in the Middle Ages, all the towns had their own fields and nearly every family held land in them. The writer who described the fire at Dorchester in 1613 said that 'it unfortunately hapned in the time of harvest, when people were much busied in the reaping of their Corne, and the Towne most emptyest.' Regulations in the manor court book of Weymouth show the rural flavour of urban life. The town common was stinted, that is to say each tenant could graze only a limited number of animals on it. Owners of pigs were to keep them from wandering in the streets. Those holding strips on the arable fields had to maintain the

Hitts House, Beaminster. There are no pointed gables or finials, but, that apart, this seventeenth century house shows no Renaissance influence. There has been an extension, but the house was never symmetrical and the windows are mullioned. The shell canopy is eighteenth century.

hedges and scour the ditches where their land adjoined streets, roads, tracks or the common.

Towns had the right to hold markets and fairs, and these brought business as well as income from tolls and fines. Each town had regulations, which were intended in the main to protect its own citizens. People selling butter or fish at Weymouth had to bring their goods straight to the open market, and at Poole, fishermen had to display their fish in the market for a full hour, before offering them elsewhere. An official called the ale-conner enforced the assizes of ale and bread, tasting the drink to assess its quality and checking weights and measures generally. Perhaps the main concern was to prevent outsiders from stealing business. In 1629 the shoemakers of Dorchester complained that 'diuers shoomakers that haue no standings graunted vnto them by the Towne doe bring base ware to this market and sell the same in buy corners, to the great damage of the Shoomakers of this Burough.' The intruders, three men from Cerne Abbas, were ordered to leave.

Running a market was not expensive. Weymouth paid a man to clean from time to time, and he needed a broom. The rope for the weighing beam was replaced occasionally. A new bushel measure for corn once cost 3s 4d, while another time the old one was repaired for 8d.

Some idea of the importance of a town's market can be gained from the size of its market place. That at Lyme Regis is minute. Given the importance of the place, Poole's is small. Blandford's is large, but only Bridport has the long wide streets needed for large numbers of stalls.

We have already seen that Dorchester had many tradesmen and craftsmen. At Weymouth, late 16th and early 17th century legal documents mention the following: mariner, lighterman, gunner, ships' carpenter, carpenter and joiner, wheelwright, cooper, mason, glazier, hellier, blacksmith, brassier, weaver, felt maker, fuller, tanner, glover, wool draper, mercer, tailor, shoemaker, brewer, miller, innkeeper, ostler, vintner, victualler, chandler, butcher, baker, surgeon, attorney, clerk, yeoman, husbandman. An incomplete list of 1617 shows three trades outnumbering all the rest; there were 14 tailors, 17 butchers and 14 ships' carpenters. The fact that the town was a port might explain the large number of butchers. Even during Lent they were allowed to sell beef and pork 'for provision of shippinge'.

The towns went on improving their status, with Poole still in the lead. Its Great Charter granted by Queen Elizabeth in 1568 marked the end of centuries of step by step progress towards self-government. In the first place, the town gained almost complete independence from its lord of the manor. Even more important, it became a county, separate from the rest of Dorset. At the time, there were only 16 other corporate counties in England. Poole also had an admiralty court held 'tyme owt of mynde', in fact since 1364. The court exercised jurisdiction over the northern part of the harbour and 'from the North haven pynte as farre to seaward as a humber barrell maie be seen and descried in the sea.' It dealt with pirates, at least after the days when the leading townsfolk were in league with them. It also prosecuted fishermen who dredged for oysters out of season or who used small mesh nets to the 'distruction of the small ffrye of fyshe.' As admiral of the port, the mayor of Poole was allowed a share of the profits from wrecks and anything found floating in the sea, including 'any dead bodye havinge uppon or about hyme any gold, silver, jewell, or other ritches.'

Other places also obtained charters during this period. In 1630 Dorchester at last acquired a mayor, one of the signs that a town had gained some status. He headed a Common Council consisting of two bailiffs, six aldermen and six capital burgesses. There was also a merchant guild which divided itself into clothiers, ironmongers, fishmongers, shoemakers and skinners. Other trades had to fit in as best they could, the fishmongers, for example, admitting carpenters, masons, brewers, butchers and fletchers.

King Charles Inn, Poole, ca. 1600. At first glance this looks a traditional timber framed building. However, it is nearly symmetrical and has an attempt at a classical doorway.

Wimborne was given a charter of incorporation in 1563 and Blandford in 1605, but neither place had a mayor. Sherborne was never incorporated, though in 1537 the minute suburb of Castleton became a borough. It was the smallest in England.

Towns made at least some attempts to keep themselves pure. The citizens of Weymouth were forbidden to leave their filth on the 'keys', in the streets or in the harbour. Brewers were also forbidden to dump their waste in the streets. Sometimes the town required a public service as a condition for a grant of land, as in 1624 when a new occupant agreed to make a gutter for a stream which 'nowe doth pass under the house of Robert Wiltshire deceased.'

Law and order were maintained as cheaply as possible. The constables, unwilling part-timers, were unpaid and served only for a year. Punishments were sharp, but inexpensive to administer. Poole had a pillory in Pillory Street, now renamed Market Close. There were stocks and a lock-up behind the Town Cellars, with a conking stool nearby. Conking, plouncing or ducking was a way of punishing women scolds. In 1631 the Dorchester justices decreed that Mary Tuxbery 'for scoulding at the sargences when they did goe about for mersments is ordered to be plownsed when the weather is warmer.' Prison sentences were rare, as they meant keeping evil-doers at the public expense. Prison was for debtors, who were expected to pay for their own keep, though in 1601 Poole made this arrangement:

> It is ordeyned, condiscended and agreed that from henceforthe the inhibytants of this towne whose names are heere under written eu'ie one of them accordinge to ther dwellings shall bestowe one after another daie by daie as they shalbe appointed one meales meate towards the releife of the prisoner now in the gaiole duringe such tyme as he shall remayne ther.

The town treasurers were called 'bailiffs'. Usually there were two. They collected the town's income in coin and distributed it in the same way. At Poole, the money was kept in the Town Box, which had a multiple lock so that several people had to be present when it was opened.

In 1493 Poole's income was £17 14s 0d, and this increased to about £40 a year by the early seventeenth century. Weymouth's income was £41 18s 11d in 1590–1 and £238 10s 7d in 1615–6, but there was no steady increase. Receipts were £132 14s 8d in 1598–8 and £38 3s 5¾d the following year. Sales of land might account for the wilder fluctuations.

Since rents were an important source of income, towns bought as much property as they could. Melcombe Regis's rentals were 18s 7d in 1579 and well over £20 by the early 17th century. The ports made money from their harbours. Poole charged keyage for moorings, hallage for storage in the town cellars, prisage for weighing goods on the town beam, boomage levied on ships according to their tonnage, and 6d a ton for either loading or unloading ballast. There were customs duties as well. Weymouth collected £20 1s 0d in 1596–7 and £139 in 1623, though the yield in 1602–3 was only £5 10s 0d.

Towns spent some money keeping their property in order. 'Glassinge the towne hall wyndowes' cost Weymouth 5s 6d and 'mending ye locke of the Hall' 4d. Sometimes there was an extraordinary expense, as when Poole built a gun platform in 1524. A great deal was spent winning the goodwill of people who mattered to the town. At different times, Blandford paid 3s 'for a gallon of wine bestowed on Sir Warwick Heal', 19s 'for wine and shugar "Bishop's Visitation"' and £1 17s 6d for 'a shugar loaf and a whole sheep presented to ye judges'. Even a gift of a deer from a nobleman led to expense, for there had to be a return present and a feast. 'Spending a buck' given by Lord Suffolk cost £2 8s 7d.

Like the Lord Mayor of London, the Mayor of Poole also had his annual banquet, one such feast costing £10 2s 7d at a time when the town's annual income was about £40.

There was some industrial growth in this period. By the late 16th century copperas and alum were being mined on Brownsea Island and along the coast between Parkstone and what is now Bournemouth. Much of the sand in today's beaches was released into the sea as a result of this work. Copperas, which is decomposed iron pyrites, was used to make ink and dyes and in the tanning of leather. Alum is a dye fixative.

Sir Walter Raleigh brought tobacco from Virginia and, indeed, it was at Sherborne that a servant is said to have extinguished him, when he found him smoking. By the early 17th century, smoking had become so popular that many pipes were needed. There was a perfect clay for making them on the heathland of the Isle of Purbeck, which was now exploited. It became known as 'pipe clay', though another name for it was 'ball clay', perhaps because it was dug with a spade called a 'tubal'.

The Isle of Portland contains one of the finest building stones in the world. It has few joints or bedding planes, so masons can carve it in any direction, it resists the weather and smoke, and it looks beautiful. For a long time Portland stone was not much appreciated outside its immediate area, but in the reign of James I, Inigo Jones used it for the royal banqueting hall in Whitehall. Later in the century, Wren used it for his London churches, St Paul's alone taking a million cubic feet. Much of the stone was quarried on the cliffs and lowered directly into boats. In 1635 Peter Mundy, a visitor to Portland, reported, 'There were about 200 workmen, some hewing out of the Cliffe above, some squareinge, some carryeing down, others ladinge. Some stones were ready squared and formed of 9, 10 and 11 tons weight.'

The rope and net industries of west Dorset had made a good start in the Middle Ages, but they stagnated in the 16th century. The people of Burton Bradstock started some rope walks and the citizens of Bridport petitioned against them. The government took the misguided view that the Bridport industries must be protected, if the navy was to be sure of its ropes, so in 1530 it prohibited rope making in any place within five miles of the town. That injured the countryside without bringing prosperity to the town itself. Here, the guilds imposed their dead hand, regulating prices and output and limiting the number of apprentices a man might have. Meanwhile, the harbour at West Bay filled with silt and fell into disrepair. In 1623 the townsfolk tried to raise £3,000 to put the harbour in order, but they managed only £67. That would have gone nowhere in restoring the harbour, but they had a school which had lain empty for years for want of a master, so they used the interest on the money to pay one.

The English woollen industry grew remarkably during the 15th and 16th centuries and exports of finished cloth rose twentyfold. Dorset, however, enjoyed only a small part of this prosperity, which may seem surprising since it was a major wool producing area. The problem was that Dorset wool was not of the first quality. Further, the best of the yarn spun from it was sent to Somerset and Wiltshire, which meant the Dorset weavers could make only coarse cloth, like 'kersies' and 'Dorset dozens'. Much of it was exported to Normandy and Brittany where the people, being 'of a base disposition', could afford nothing better. Then, late in the 16th century, the New Draperies became popular. They were lighter than the traditional cloths, having silk or cotton warps. Dorset's weavers could not cope with such a radical change of fashion and it was East Anglia that took the market.

A new industry appeared in east Dorset. In 1622 Abraham Case settled in Shaftesbury where he found thousands of sheep's horns going to waste. He sliced them into thin discs and covered them with linen which he embroidered, so making attractive buttons. Case buttons became popular. Charles I had some on the silk waistcoat he wore to his execution.

11

ELIZABETHAN SEAMEN

In the early 16th century England hardly counted as a maritime power, yet by the time Anne, the last of the Stuarts, died in 1714, Great Britain had a large navy, a merchant fleet that traded all over the world and a thriving colonial empire. Dorset helped achieve this success in various ways.

It was Queen Elizabeth's father, Henry VIII, who laid the foundations of England's naval power, not only by building warships like the *Mary Rose*, but also by constructing a string of artillery castles along the coast from the Humber to Milford Haven. They were formidable defences, since by the 16th century there were guns that could throw heavy shot well over a mile.

In Dorset, Henry built a castle on Brownsea Island to protect the entrance to Poole Harbour. He also defended the Portland roadstead with Sandsfoot Castle, near Weymouth, and Portland Castle on the north coast of the Isle. They were two miles apart so that, between them, they covered the whole bay.

What remains of Brownsea Castle is now embedded in the foundations of a later building and much of Sandsfoot Castle has slipped into the sea, but Portland Castle is intact. It is, perhaps, the best example of this style of fortress in England. There are no towering walls as at Corfe but, instead, the building is squat and rounded. It has a casemate, or covered gun platform, and a low keep. The casemate presents a semi-circular wall to the sea, with embrasures for five guns, while four more guns were mounted on the roof. Even more guns could be put on the keep, making a third tier. Here, then, was a battleship on dry land. Moreover not only was it unsinkable, but almost indestructible, for the walls, superbly built of Portland stone, are 14 feet thick. The cost of the building was £4,964 18s 10¼d. which may have been proceeds from the dissolution of the monasteries.

None of these castles saw much action against foreigners but once, during the reign of Elizabeth, Brownsea Castle fired on a Poole vessel, killing two of her crew.

England's naval power grew dramatically under Elizabeth, and not the least of the Queen's achievements was the taming of her own pirates.

Many of the English pirates were from Dorset, and they were popular in the county. At sea they were merciless and brutal, but on land they were jovial, entertaining and generous. One of their favourite haunts was Studland, the gateway to the Isle of Purbeck. When a 'man-of-war' appeared in the bay, folk came from miles in the hope of receiving presents and in the certainty of making some good bargains.

It was the royal officials who were most favoured by the pirates. Clinton Atkinson once gave Francis Hawley 'two sugar loaves, about twelve pounds of ginger, a fair pair of hand-irons and tongs, half a dozen fine stools and a fine little waggon.' Hawley was deputy to the Vice-Admiral of Purbeck, no less a person than Sir Christopher Hatton, Queen Elizabeth's Chancellor. Humbler folk might also benefit. When Stephen Heynes captured a cargo of cottons he decked out 30 of Studland's poor, some in white and some in green. The pirates' serious business, though, was with merchants like Thomas Perkins of Wareham. It was a pleasure to deal with pirates, for they rarely haggled over the prices of their own goods and gladly paid more than the going rate for supplies. All transactions completed, the pirates and the local men adjourned to William Munday's pub where they caroused through the night.

When Queen Elizabeth came to the throne there was little she could do about pirates and perhaps their activities did not worry her unduly. After all, while she was still a princess, Admiral Seymour had given her some lavish presents that he had obtained from pirates. But it gradually became clear that England and Spain were drifting into war and that England would need all the friends she could find. Her pirates, though, were making enemies everywhere, so Elizabeth decided to suppress them.

Putting down piracy was like eradicating a mafia. The pirates had been wise in their generosity, for all along the coast they could count on the friendship of vice-admirals, justices of the peace, mayors, controllers of customs and most of the ordinary people. Nor was there any stigma attached to piracy. When the mayor of Christchurch was asked to explain why he had gone aboard a pirate vessel he replied, in all innocence, 'For good company and to make money.'

Elizabeth turned to the few men on whom she could rely. Chief among them were the judges of the High Court of Admiralty, notably the oddly named Sir Julius Caesar who would question a lying witness like a needle probing a decayed tooth, at the same time dropping hints about the agonies of the rack. One move, then, was to make sure that

Portland Castle.

all pirate trials took place in London where the end was likely to be the gallows at Wapping and not some 'composition' between magistrates and accused. Locally, support was less sure, but even in Dorset there was Sir Henry Ashley of Wimborne St Giles who would hunt pirates just for the pleasure of the chase. Such men sat on the Commissions for Piracy which referred captives to the High Court of Admiralty. Also, the navy was growing and its smaller ships were employed against pirates. In 1583 the *Bark Talbot* and the *Unicorn* caught seven 'men-of-war' off the Dorset coast.

There remained the problem of men like Sir Richard Rogers. He was connected by marriage with the Vice-Admiral of Dorset, Viscount Howard of Bindon, he was Lord of the Manor of Bryanston, he was a Justice of the Peace and he was, at various times Deputy Lord Lieutenant and High Sheriff of Dorset. He was also a promoter of pirates.

In 1577 Captain Courte Higgenbert's 'man-of-war' was driven ashore in Mupe Bay. Sir Richard rescued her cargo, refloated her, revictualled her and sent her on her way. For this, he was summoned before the Privy Council. The Council faced a dilemma. Sir Richard had to be cured of his bad habits but, at the same time, he must not be alienated. Without the support of men like Rogers, the Queen was powerless. The solution was a fine of £100. It was enough to show that the Crown meant business but gave Sir Richard cause to feel grateful that he had escaped so lightly. It is possible, too, that he considered the likely fate of Protestant landowners under Spanish rule and decided he would do well to rally to the Queen. Whatever the reason, Elizabeth had, from then on, no subject more loyal than Sir Richard Rogers. He stumped round Dorset inspecting defences, he drilled the Blandford levies and he even sat on the Commission for Piracy.

As friction with Spain increased, so Dorset prepared for war, though without much enthusiasm. It had long been the duty of England's citizens to organise their own defence, and Elizabeth's Privy Council reminded them of this in 1558. Everyone was to own at least a bow, while those who could afford arquebuses were encouraged to buy them. There was to be regular target practice, with military exercises after church on Sundays and holy days. Seaports were to take censuses of their ships, stating tonnage, weapons and crews. Everywhere, lists were to be compiled of able-bodied men and their weapons. These lists revealed serious deficiencies, Poole's levies, for example, forming but a 'weak and simple company' with only one corselet between them. It seems that the military exercises were neglected, since in 1572 the Privy Council instructed Weymouth that any man who refused to take part in them should be douched with sea water. In 1586 the twin towns of Weymouth and Melcombe Regis asked the government for ten or a dozen guns to protect their harbour, though when there was a bill for a ton of gunpowder, many of the citizens refused to pay their share.

When Philip II sent the Armada to conquer England in 1588, the coastal towns were ordered to provide ships. Lyme Regis sent two, and Weymouth and Melcombe Regis sent the *John* of 90 tons and the *Reprisal* of 60 tons which were to join the fleet, while six smaller vessels were to act as coasters. Poole was instructed to send a ship of 60 tons and a pinnace. The town answered the Privy Council with a reasoned letter which began, 'Our obedient duties unto your Honours in most humble wise remembered', but went on to refuse the ship and pinnace on the grounds of poverty. Henry Carew made a private contribution to the war when he paid a ship's captain £10, but Carew was a Catholic and the money was a bribe to persuade the captain not to put to sea against the Armada. Carew should have saved his money. The little ships from the Channel ports took no part in the fighting, but left it all to the Queen's ships and the Londoners. This was wise. Even the doyenne of Poole's merchant fleet, the *Castell of Comfort*, mounted only six light guns. She had two sakers, which were 6 pounders, two minyons which were $3\frac{3}{4}$ pounders and two falcons which were $2\frac{1}{8}$ pounders. Assuming the guns were distributed equally to port and starboard, the ship could fire a broadside of just under twelve pounds. A single shot from one of the larger Spanish guns weighed 60 pounds.

The Armada sailed along the English coast, the people of Dorset watching it anxiously, for they could not know that King Philip's orders precluded it from attempting a landing until it had escorted the Duke of Parma's army from the Low Countries. There was some additional excitement for Weymouth when the *San Salvador*, one of the Spaniards' most powerful ships, appeared in the bay. Her powder magazine had exploded, reducing her to a battered hulk, full of maimed and burned men. The people of Weymouth looted her.

Though Dorset's contribution to the defeat of the Armada was hardly glorious, her seamen did play a significant part in the war as a whole. They did so by privateering. The suppression of piracy had been a shrewd blow to many adventurous Englishmen, but now the war brought an open season for Spaniards. Since Philip II deployed the bulk of his navy to convoy the treasure ships from America, he could do little to protect ordinary merchant vessels and these fell prey to English privateers. Privateering on its own was an uncertain road to wealth. The entrepreneur who did best was the merchant who sent his ship on a conventional trading voyage, but armed it well in the hope that it might pick up a prize. The trading guaranteed a basic profit while the prize, if any, was a bonus. Spain's merchant fleet dwindled year by year, so that when the war ended in 1604 most of her trade was conducted by foreigners, Dorset men among them.

A good example of a privateering trader was George Somers of Lyme Regis. Though from a humble family, he did so well in his profession that he turned himself into a landed gentleman, acquired a knighthood and became Admiral of the West Virginia Company's fleet. It was Somers who discovered the Bermudas, which he did by being shipwrecked on them. One of his companions, another Dorset man called Silvester Jourdan, compiled a lively account of their adventures and it was reading this which inspired Shakespeare to write *The Tempest*.

Ordinary trade continued during Elizabeth's reign, in spite of piracy and war. To appreciate its scale, we have only to look at the Cobb at Lyme Regis and reflect that this little breakwater created one of the busiest havens in the south of England. A ship of 1,000 tons was, in those days, a leviathan. There were yards capable of building such vessels, but it was unlikely that anyone would want them. The East India Company learnt a hard lesson when, in 1609, its *Trades Increase* of 1,000 tons was lost on her maiden voyage, along with a valuable cargo. Nor was it just a question of spreading risks, since the larger the ship, the longer she had to wait for a full cargo and this would only arrive in a trickle. Everywhere, the roads serving the ports were so poor that most goods travelled on pack animals, while at Lyme Regis the gradients were so steep that no wheeled traffic at all could enter the town. As a result, ships were small. In 1578, the 19 ships based on Lyme Regis varied in size from 110 tons to eight. In 1591 Poole had 21 ships, the largest being the *Castell of Comfort* of 70 tons and the smallest *The Peter* of 14 tons. Poole's total tonnage was little more than 800.

Most of Dorset's trade was coastal and cross-Channel. Poole had links with the Channel Islands, and Weymouth with Brittany. Poole imported canvas, wine, fish and fruit, while exporting raw wool, woollen cloth, lead, tin, corn, flour and beer. The Weymouth mayoral accounts of 1579 record duty paid on 'certayn canvas and a pocket of hoppes', 'ij puncheons of pruyns', 'tenne tonnes of Iron' and by 'ij Brytayne Barkes laden wth sallte'. A similar list comes from Lyme Regis, but there is also mention of gold dust and 'elephants' teeth', while in 1595 the mayor of the town presented the Marquis of Winchester with a 'fair box of marmelades gilted, a barrel of conserves, oranges and lemons, and potatoes.'

Though they remained small, ships had much improved since the Middle Ages. They had more masts, with more advanced rigging, so that even crossing the Atlantic became commonplace. One result was that trade with Newfoundland also became important. Cabot had discovered the island in 1497 and reported shoals of cod so huge that they slowed his vessel. When English fishermen first went to the Grand Banks is not known, though it might have been before Cabot's voyage. The Poole records of 1528 mention Newfoundland fish. Then, in 1583, Sir Humphrey Gilbert annexed Newfoundland for Queen Elizabeth. He had with him a Poole man, one Christopher Farewell, who came home to a fine of £30. He was Poole's senior bailiff and had abandoned his duties without permission from the mayor.

At first, the ships each took two crews, one to fish and one to dry and salt the catches, but soon there were permanent settlers to do the preserving. That meant increased trade, for the settlers needed supplies of all kinds, even food, since most of Newfoundland is infertile.

The normal routine for the trade is shown in instructions to the captain of the *Diamond* of Lyme Regis in 1608. He was to leave for Newfoundland in March and load with cod. He was then to sell the fish in 'Espayne or Portingall' where he was to purchase whatever cargo seemed best, and return by the autumn. The Catholics of Iberia welcomed salt cod, and, indeed, it is still a favourite with the Portuguese who claim they have 365 ways of cooking it. For their part, the English much appreciated Iberian wines and fruit.

12

THE PURITANS

The defeat of the Spanish Armada meant an end to the danger from Catholics, but as that faded the Protestant extremists gained converts, especially in the towns. They were known as Puritans and were of two kinds. Some, who were followers of Calvin, wished to form churches which would be quite separate from the Church of England; most of them were either Presbyterians or Independents. Other Puritans remained loyal to the Church of England, but wished to change her from within.

In daily life, all Puritans had much in common. They dressed plainly. They followed, or took care to seem to follow, strict moral codes. They worked hard and if they made money they saw it as a sign of divine favour. They despised trivial amusements, the people of Dorchester for example dismissing puppet shows with, 'We have noe waste mony for such idle things.' In church, the separatists favoured plain buildings and plain services, while the Anglican Puritans allowed a certain amount of ornament and ritual. All Puritan clergy preached interminable sermons.

Dorset's most famous Puritan was the Rev John White, rector of Holy Trinity and of St Peter's, Dorchester, from 1606 to 1648. White, the son of an Oxfordshire farmer, was born in 1575. He went to school at Winchester and then studied at New College Oxford, where he came under the influence of Calvinists. He absorbed some of their ideas, but he remained loyal to the Anglican faith. At Dorchester he showed he was no extremist, since he wore the surplice, bought communion plate and provided a new carpet for his communion table. Moreover, he dismissed the Puritan separatists as 'men of fiery and turbulent spirits, that walk in a cross way out of distemper of mind.'

On taking up his duties, White found that Dorchester 'possessed anything but a pious and estimable reputation.' This he was determined to change and the town records show his influence. In 1631 Joe Kay and Nicholas Sims were sent to prison, their offence being that they 'did play at sermon time and laughe, and Sims did stick Kay a box on the ear and carry themselves very unreverently.' In 1632 Ursula Bull was fined one shilling for not attending church, her only excuse being that 'she was amending her stockings.' One Sunday in January 1634, J. Hoskins was shivering in church so he went to a friend's house to warm himself. He then found a bull which he baited with a dog. He was back in church before the service ended, but he had been missed and was fined a shilling.

In 1613, White was helped rather than hindered by a fire which destroyed much of Dorchester. The town's leaders admitted that in the past they had done little for the poor, but after the fire, 'men's bowels began to yearn in compassion towards them, studying how to do some good work for their relief.' Almshouses were built. There was a hospital where poor children were catechised and taught how to spin and, along with it, a brewhouse to earn it money. The Free School was rebuilt, with a public library on an upper floor. Among the books were Speed's *History and Maps of England* and, inevitably, Foxe's *Booke of Martyrs* which describes in vivid detail the burning of the Protestant heretics under Mary Tudor.

Religion was less dour in other parts of Dorset. A clergyman who came to hold a service at Plush had to chase chickens out of the pulpit and remove a bag of ferrets. Thomas Fuller, rector of Broadwindsor, would make his congregations roar with laughter. He was a distinguished man who wrote several books, including the lively *Worthies of England*, and who became chaplain to the Cavalier armies. He was, in his own way, as devout as John White.

As well as establishing a Puritan régime in Dorchester, White encouraged emigration to North America. Virginia had been established by 1607, while the most famous emigrants of all, the Pilgrim Fathers, had sailed to New England in 1620. White was interested in emigration for several reasons. One was practical. As we have seen, vessels going to the Grand Banks for cod had to carry two crews, one to fish and the other to dry and salt the catches, but settlers could undertake the work of the second group, reducing costs considerably. Also, in the 1620s there was a depression in the woollen industry, which caused unemployment. White blamed what he imagined to be over-population and believed that emigration would ease the problem. However, a third motive was far more important than the other two. As White put it, 'The most eminent and desirable end of planting is the propagation of religion.'

There were three strands to the religious thinking. In the first place, White was concerned for the fishermen who, 'being usually upon their voyages nine or ten months in the year were left without means of instruction.' Secondly there were the American Indians to convert. White remarked, with touching optimism, 'Withall, commerce and example of

Pulpit, 1632, Bradford Abbas church. Due to Puritan influence, the sermon became an important part of the church service. For that reason, there are many fine pulpits of the early seventeenth century.

our course of living cannot but in time breed civility among them and that, by God's blessing, may make way for religion consequently and for the saving of their souls.' Finally, the New World would provide a haven for those who wished to follow White's own brand of moderate puritanism, free from the oppression of the king and his High Church bishops.

In 1624 White called a meeting of like-minded men at Dorchester, a gathering that was later referred to as 'the Planters' Parliament'. This was followed by the formation of the Dorchester Company, composed of about 200 clergy, gentry and merchants. The very same year the Company despatched the 50 ton *Fellowship* on a fishing expedition and, in pursuance of White's plans, the ship carried a small group of settlers, which it left at Cape Ann, on Massachusetts Bay. Further expeditions followed in 1625 and 1626, but all three lost money. The Dorchester adventurers sold their ships and wound up their company.

White, however, was unwilling to abandon a noble cause, and he could not ignore the settlement at Cape Ann. In 1628 John Endicott went out in the *Abigail* to become the colony's first governor and further reinforcements were despatched in 1629. Fugitives arrived from the Pilgrim Fathers' settlement of New Plymouth, among them the Rev John Lyford. Lyford had had a bastard son before marrying and his wife complained that 'she could keep no maids but he would be meddling with them'. His worst crime, though, was to insist on administering the rites of the Church of England. The Pilgrims expelled both Lyford and his friend John Oldham, the latter receiving a valedictory 'bob upon the bumme by every musketeer'.

Meanwhile, more important moves were afoot in England. Merchants from several parts of the country, notably London, formed the New England Company, later renamed the Massachusetts Bay Company. Dorset men were only a minority in the new company, but White still had an important part to play by recruiting from his own sphere of influence, which extended into south Somerset.

The folk that White attracted were all from what Thomas Fuller called 'the temperate zone between greatness and want'. The sailors among them were master mariners, most of the countryfolk were yeomen, while the townspeople were skilled artisans, such as coopers, tanners and masons. Several were relatives of clergy and White took care to include 'two Reverend and Godly Ministers of the Word'.

These people must have had various reasons for leaving 'the smoke of their own chimneys'. Though not poor, they had cause to fear poverty, since Dorset's woollen industry was in decline and there had been a run of bad harvests, as well as epidemics of smallpox and typhus. Perhaps some were swayed by White's descriptions of New England. He was especially enthusiastic about the wine that could be made from wild grapes 'as good as any that are found in France by humane culture'. A promise of freehold land was a powerful incentive. This land was going to be awarded in proportion to the amounts contributed to the expedition, but the minimum was 50 acres per family. Only a few of the settlers have left any record of their views and they stated that their motive was religion, though one would hardly expect disciples of John White to say anything different.

In March 1630 the Massachusetts Bay Company despatched a fleet of ships carrying 700 settlers. The first contingent to leave included John White's protégés, sailing in the *Mary and John*. Aboard were twelve bachelors, 27 married couples, 72 children and an unknown number of assorted animals. At 400 tons the ship was unusually large, so the passengers had a reasonable amount of space and a fair crossing.

Troubles began on the other side. Captain Thomas Squibb had contracted to go to the mouth of the Charles river, but he declined to risk his large vessel among the rocks of Massachusetts Bay and forced his passengers to disembark on a barren headland known as Nantasket Point. Eventually, they made their way to Mattapan Neck where they founded a settlement which they called 'Dorchester' and a church which they named 'The Daughter of John White'.

The country was far from hospitable. It was too late to sow corn and, though there was plenty of game, the settlers did not know how to catch it. They spent the long winter in shelters like Indian tepees, where they suffered from scurvy, cold and hunger. It was lucky that in February a ship arrived carrying supplies. The adults survived the winter, to enjoy their freehold land and their religious liberty. It was the children who died.

13

CIVIL WAR AND REBELLION

The English Civil War is sometimes portrayed as a struggle between King and Parliament, but, in fact, Charles I had surrendered many of his powers to Parliament before a shot was fired. As long as Parliament was united, it had the king at its mercy, but it split over religion, and it was this dispute which led to war. On one side were the mainstream Anglicans, who accepted the King as their leader because he was head of their church. On the other side were the Puritans, led by what was left of Parliament after its Anglican members had fled. The Puritans were themselves divided into two main sects, the Presbyterians and the Independents. The Anglicans are usually called Royalists or Cavaliers, while the Puritans are known as Parliamentarians or Roundheads.

The two Puritan factions fought side by side from the outbreak of war in 1642 until they were victorious in 1645. They then fell out, starting a second Civil War that was fought in 1648. The Independents won and their leading general, Oliver Cromwell, governed the country as Lord Protector.

The war was fought at two levels. There were the campaigns by the principal armies, which had the mastery of the entire country as their final aim. In addition, there were local struggles, with men fighting for the control of particular areas. Dorset's war was of the second kind and there was no major battle in the county.

Like most of west and south-west England, Dorset was mainly Royalist, but merchants tended to be Puritans, so Dorchester and the seaport towns of Poole, Melcombe Regis and Lyme Regis were Roundhead enclaves. Weymouth, another port, was Royalist, but that was because it never agreed with its twin, Melcombe Regis, about anything. Broadly speaking, the fighting went through two phases. In the early years, the Cavaliers reduced all the Roundhead strongholds, except Poole and Lyme Regis. In the later years, the Roundheads took control of the county, following the victories of their main armies elsewhere.

Dorchester, which had long been dominated by John White, was a bastion of the Puritan faith. In his *History of the Great Rebellion* the Royalist Edward Hyde wrote, 'No place was more deeply imbued with the rigid piety of the Puritans', and he added that it was 'the magazine whence other places were supplied with the principles of Rebellion.' The citizens set about turning their spiritual fortress into a military one by spending £20,000 on defences. This included digging a gun emplacement into the bank of Maumbury Rings, to cover the Weymouth road. It was a sad blow to morale when Colonel William Strode inspected the defences and reported, 'Those works might keep out the Cavaliers about half an hour.' He claimed that 'the royal soldiers made nothing of running up walls twenty foot high.'

In 1643, Lord Carnarvon appeared before the town, and it surrendered without firing a shot. Carnarvon promised there would be no looting, but then Prince Maurice, the king's nephew, arrived and his men plundered at will. John White's house suffered more than most. Thereafter, Dorchester was an open town, with the armies of both sides coming and going as they pleased.

There was stronger Puritan resistance elsewhere. Poole began by flushing out its Royalists, notably the mayor, Henry Harbin, and then strengthened its defences. Parliament, realising the value of having a friendly town deep in enemy territory, sent money and munitions, so the place was well prepared when the Earl of Crawford appeared before it in 1643. The siege was remarkable only because of a piece of trickery. An officer of the garrison, Francis Sydenham, said he was willing to betray the town in return for £40 on account, with more money to follow along with a ship and a pardon. The plan was that on the night when Sydenham was captain of the guard, he would open the gate and sound a horn as a signal. Royalist cavalry would then rush the town. In front of the gate was an outwork known as a 'half moon', with, across its entrance, chains that could be 'drawn up at pleasure'. The horn sounded and the attackers charged into the half moon, only to realise that the chains had been drawn up behind them. Most of them escaped because the defenders could not depress their guns enough to fire on them, but the Royalists did not attempt the town again.

Poole troubled the Royalists for the rest of the war. Its privateers preyed on their shipping, and in 1644 its garrison skirmished with Lord Inchquin's Irish Regiment, attacked the Queen's Regiment near Blandford and captured a convoy which was carrying £3,000 of Prince Rupert's money near Dorchester. In 1646 it helped take Corfe Castle.

When Prince Maurice attacked Lyme Regis in 1644, he promised his men that the capture of the place would be 'breakfast work', but the siege lasted eight weeks. The Cavaliers tried to set fire to thatched roofs with flaming arrows and red hot cannon balls. When all else failed, they resorted to witchcraft. Among the defenders, Robert Blake distinguished himself, as did Captain Davey who resolutely held one of the outlying forts when all the others had fallen. The women of Lyme brought ammunition to the men, loaded the muskets, and dressed like men themselves to give a false idea of the strength of the garrison. There was no danger of the town running out of supplies, for they came in by sea. Eventually, the Parliamentary commander-in-chief, the Earl of Essex, approached and Maurice raised the siege. Robert Blake was rewarded with the rank of colonel and went on to become General at Sea under Cromwell.

Two places that suffered badly were Beaminster and Wareham. Prince Maurice came to Beaminster in 1643, with a motley army that included Cornish, Irish and French units. One night they brawled, someone fired a musket and a thatched roof caught fire. Soon, the little town was ablaze. 'It was a wild fire and the wind directly with the towne, so the whole towne was destroyed in two hours.'

Wareham's misfortunes began when men from the Poole garrison raided in 1643. They took away prisoners, ammunition and many of the goods that were due to be sold in the market the following day. In 1644, Anthony Ashley Cooper took the town for Parliament, lost it and then recaptured it. Even after that, Colonel Cromwell, a Royalist this one, raided Wareham and carried the Parliamentary Governor to Corfe Castle. Cooper was so exasperated that he urged Parliament to destroy the town entirely. 'There can be no arguments against demolishing it,' he said, 'being extremely meanly built and the inhabitants almost all dreadful malignants.' Parliament did not take this advice.

One of the most romantic episodes of the entire Civil War was the defence of Corfe Castle in 1643. The owner of the castle, Sir John Bankes, went with the King, leaving his wife, Lady Mary, to look after their home. At first she had only five soldiers, but when the Roundheads approached, Captain Lawrence arrived with 80 men. The besiegers under Sir Walter Erle and Captain William Sydenham numbered 600.

A Royalist calling himself Mercurius Rusticus described the siege. He told how the attackers were unable to prevent a sortie by the garrison which brought in eight cows and a bull. He also described Sir Walter Erle reconnoitring the castle by clambering over the sides of its hill disguised in a bear skin, a most unlikely story. The attackers had cannon, but they were not powerful enough to breach the walls, so they built themselves a 'sow' and a 'boar', which were covered battering rams. They did little damage, because the defenders shot the legs of the men using them.

Siege of Corfe Castle, 1643. The guns were not heavy enough to breach the walls. (Dorset County Museum)

Then 150 sailors arrived, bringing scaling ladders and hand grenades. Erle gave them drink and told them that the first man over the walls would have £20, the second £19 and so on, down to £1. The sailors chose to attack the upper ward which, being the strongest part of the castle, was held by the fewest defenders. The ladders were mounted and the agile sailors swarmed up them. On the walls were Lady Mary, her daughters, her maids and just five men, who poured down such a barrage of stones and red hot cinders that the sailors fled.

After six weeks the army of Prince Maurice approached, so the Roundheads raised the siege at once. Sydenham's dinner had been laid in the church, but he left it untouched.

'Brave Dame Mary' was the heroine of the Royalist cause, but it should be pointed out that since the Roundheads lacked an adequate siege train, they had to use medieval methods of attack. Under those circumstances, the odds of more than one to ten were quite favourable to the defence.

Corfe was besieged again in 1646, this time by a force under the Governor of Poole, Colonel Bingham. Lady Mary was still in the castle, but there were senior Royalist officers as well, and they took charge. One of them, Colonel Pittman, realised that the war was as good as over and was unhappy about men dying in a futile fight to the finish.

107

He pretended to bring in reinforcements, but they were Roundheads in disguise and the castle fell. Afterwards, the castle was 'slighted', or damaged beyond repair.

Sherborne, like Corfe was a Royalist stronghold. The Earl of B. lford captured it for Parliament in 1642, and was preparing to destroy it when his sister, Lady Digby, who was the wife of the owner, told him that if he carried out his plan, 'he would find his sister's bones buried in the ruins.' Bedford desisted, so in 1645 Fairfax and Cromwell had to capture the castle again. This time, it was slighted thoroughly.

As the war dragged on ordinary people became more and more angry at the damage they suffered, so much so that in 1645 many in Wiltshire and Dorset formed armed bands to protect themselves. They were known as 'clubmen'. On one of their banners they wrote:

> If you offer to plunder or take our cattel,
> Rest assured we will bid you battel.

There were mass meetings on Badbury Rings, at Sturminster Newton and elsewhere, which sent delegates to both sides. The Royalists, who by then were losing the war, gave assurances, but the Roundheads were in no mood to bargain, especially as the New Model Army was in the area. After some scuffling, 2,000 clubmen took refuge in the Iron Age fortress of Hambledon Hill, and here a handful of Cromwell's dragoons routed them. They killed only a dozen, but wounded many more. Cromwell wrote to Fairfax saying, 'We have taken about 300, many of which are poor, silly creatures.' Cromwell released most of his captives, keeping only the ringleaders, including the Rev Thomas Bravell of Compton Abbas who had encouraged his troops by declaring he would 'pistol them that gave back.'

Charles I was executed in 1649, after which his son Charles II was king, if only in name. He joined the Presbyterian Scots and was with them when, in 1651, Cromwell defeated them at Worcester.

Charles fled south, accompanied by a small band that arrived, eventually, at Trent in north Dorset. Charles hid in the manor house, which belonged to Colonel Francis Wyndham, a staunch Royalist. One day, he heard the bells peal and saw an excited crowd gathering in the churchyard. He was told that the villagers were celebrating, for a Roundhead trooper had arrived saying that he had killed Charles Stuart and taken the buff coat he was wearing from the corpse. 'Alas! Poor people!' said Charles.

Later, Charles failed to take ship at Charmouth, was nearly captured at Bridport and returned to Trent. In the end, he escaped at Shoreham.

Two of Dorset's most famous sons flourished during the time of the Civil War. One was Denzil Holles who came to the fore in 1629 when he was MP for Dorchester. The Commons had attacked the king over religion and taxation, so he sent a message ordering them to adjourn. The Speaker rose to comply, but Holles, with the help of another MP, held him in his chair, exclaiming 'God's wounds, you shall sit here till *we* please to rise.' For that, Holles spent some time in the Tower of London. When the Long Parliament was summoned in 1640, Holles antagonised the king and was one of the five members that Charles tried to arrest in the House of Commons in 1642.

The Civil War began badly for Parliament, so Holles moderated his tone and became one of a peace party. Later, as a Presbyterian, he opposed the Independents and criticised Cromwell so vigorously that he felt it wise to go abroad. He supported the Restoration, for which he was given a peerage, and became one of the king's most loyal subjects. The inscription on his monument in St Peter's, Dorchester, is amusing for the subtle way that it glosses over his conflicts with the Crown during his earlier years.

Anthony Ashley Cooper had an even more remarkable career. At the beginning of the war he fought for the king, but in 1644 he went over to Parliament, 'resolving to cast himself on God and to follow the dictates of a good conscience.' The realisation that the Royalists were losing may also have influenced him. Parliament made him Field Marshal General, which meant he had charge of the little army that took Wareham and Abbotsbury in 1644.

When Cromwell became Lord Protector, he invited Ashley Cooper to join his Council of State. Cromwell died in 1658, to be succeeded by his son Richard. Ashley Cooper saw that the new government could not last, so he joined others as shrewd as himself who were plotting the return of the king. After the Restoration he was made Baron Ashley and later joined the Cabal, a select group of ministers through which Charles II governed. The king said he was 'master of more law than all his judges and more divinity than all his bishops.' In 1672 Ashley Cooper became the first Earl of Shaftesbury and Lord Chancellor. The following year, though, he was out of office.

Shaftesbury was hardly a man of principle, but he was at least consistent in his distrust of Roman Catholics. As a result, he was against the accession to the throne of the king's Roman Catholic brother, James, Duke of York. This in turn meant he lost the royal favour. In 1681 he faced a charge of high treason and, though acquitted, he fled to Holland where he died in 1683.

Shaftesbury's opposition to the Duke of York led him to support the vain, ambitious but empty-headed Duke of Monmouth, and Monmouth's bid for the throne was to have appalling consequences for Dorset.

Though Charles II sired twelve illegitimate offspring his wife, Catherine of Braganza, bore him no children at all. Monmouth, the eldest of Charles's children, was born to Lucy Walter in Rotterdam in 1649. Charles was in exile at the time, following the defeat of the Cavaliers in the Civil War. At the Restoration, Charles brought the boy to England, made him a duke and spoiled him thoroughly. However, when Monmouth asked his father to make him his heir, Charles was furious, and there were no more royal favours. Monmouth then co-operated with Shaftesbury, touring the western counties to win support. He was greeted with enthusiasm everywhere so it must have seemed that most people would rather have him, the Protestant Duke, as king, than the Catholic James. In 1683 the Rye House Plot to assassinate the king was uncovered and, as Monmouth was implicated, he fled into exile.

Charles II died in 1685, whereupon his brother became king. Monmouth made his own bid for the throne that same year. He landed at Lyme Regis on 11th June, where he was greeted with cries of 'A Monmouth! A Monmouth and the Protestant religion!' Within a few days he had over 1,500 recruits.

The first engagement was at Bridport. Lord Grey, who commanded the cavalry, occupied the town for a while, but fled without a proper fight when the local militia attacked. Monmouth should have sacked Grey on the spot, but he allowed him to keep his command.

The rebels moved into Somerset, where Taunton declared for Monmouth. His army had now grown to between 5,000 and 6,000 foot and 1,000 horse. The men who joined were, for the most part, yeomen farmers, craftsmen and small traders. The gentry held aloof, and without them Monmouth was doomed.

After some futile manoeuvres, the rebels faced James's army at Sedgemoor. It made short work of Monmouth's men. The royalist second-in-command was John Churchill, who was to become Duke of Marlborough and win great battles against the armies of Louis XIV. Sedgemoor was his first victory.

Monmouth fought bravely, but fled when he saw that all was lost. He made his way towards the coast, hoping to escape by ship, as his father had done. He and three companions arrived in Dorset at Woodyates, where they left their horses. Monmouth went on his way disguised as a shepherd, but shortly afterwards, some militia pulled him out of a ditch on Horton Heath. They took him to Holt Lodge, the home of Anthony Ettrick, Recorder of Poole, who despatched him towards London, his arms tied behind his back.

House said to have been Judge Jeffreys's lodgings in Dorchester.

Monmouth pleaded for mercy, but in vain. Thomas Chafin of Chettle House wrote to his wife from London:

> I hope to be home on Saturday sennight. The late Duke of Monmouth's head was severed from his body yesterday morning on Tower Hill about ten or eleven forenoon. Lord Grey will soon be there too. Blessing to the bratts. Soe, farewell, my dearest Nan.

Meanwhile, the royalists had rounded up the fugitives from Sedgemoor, as well as some who had been guilty of nothing more than being away from home at the time of the rebellion. The judges who tried them were headed by the Lord Chief Justice, George Jeffreys. With them was the executioner Jack Ketch, who had beheaded Monmouth and who was to gain such renown that he gave his name to all others who followed him in his trade.

The sessions of 1685 became known as the 'Bloody Assize'. They began in Dorchester, where Jeffreys held his court in the Oak Room of the Antelope Hotel. There were 312 accused. Jeffreys, a vindictive man at the best of times, was in a foul mood because he was in pain from 'the stone'. He set the tone of the proceedings by telling the accused that if they were to expect mercy they must save his time by pleading guilty. Only 34 ignored his advice. Over five days 74 were sentenced to be hanged, drawn and quartered, 178 were to be transported, nine were to be fined or whipped and 54 were acquitted. Of the 34 who had pleaded not guilty, 29 were sentenced to death.

There were other sessions in other counties, but even though only one tenth of the accused came from Dorset, there were far more executions here than anywhere. The West Indian planters had seen a golden opportunity and put in an urgent plea for workers. Of the 800 sentenced to transportation, a hundred died on the voyage.

Jack Ketch carried out the hangings while the quarterings were the work of Pascha Rose, a professional butcher. To intimidate the population, the executions took place in a variety of places. Twelve men died at Lyme Regis on the very spot where Monmouth had landed. A loyal gentleman called Jones retrieved two of the heads, which he kept on pedestals in his garden. There were also executions at Bridport, Poole, Sherborne, Wareham and Weymouth. The bodies were distributed even more widely. The constable of Upper Lytchett received a delivery from Poole, together with this note from the mayor:

> I doe herby will and require you to take into your care and custody
> two quarters of the severall persons this day executed within this

towne and county and herewith sent you by Charles Barfoot of Sturminster Marshall, husbandman, and to affix them on poles or spykes in the most notable places in Upper Litchett, and hereof fale you not at your perills.

The officer to pay five shillings for carridge.

Very few wealthy people supported Monmouth, but Edmund Prideaux the younger of Forde Abbey had sent him horses and £500. He was 'given' to Jeffreys, who agreed to release him for £15,000, with a rebate of £240 for prompt payment. Azariah Pinney of Broadwindsor was deported to the West Indies, but, being of a good family, was allowed to go as a free emigrant. He made a fortune as his father's agent, selling Dorset lace and other goods.

There were plots against James II after the rebellion, as is shown by an inscription over the ice house in Charborough Park. It reads, 'Under this roof in the year 1686 a set of patriotic gentlemen of this neighbourhood concerted the great plan of the GLORIOUS REVOLUTION with the immortal King William, to whom we owe our deliverance from Popery and Slavery.' In fact, the Glorious Revolution took place in 1688, provoked by the birth of a son to James's second wife, Mary of Modena. The English upper classes had been willing to accept a Catholic king rather than risk a civil war, but a Catholic dynasty was another matter. James had a Protestant daughter, Mary, who was married to William of Orange, a grandson of Charles I and Stadholder of the United Provinces. Mary and 'Dutch' William were invited to rule as joint sovereigns.

William landed with his army at Torbay and made his cautious way towards London, passing through north Dorset. A 'rigid Papist that lived near unto Beminster' tried to poison some of his men with doctored pies, but he was well received at Sherborne Castle by John Digby, Earl of Bristol. During his stay at Sherborne, William made a proclamation assuring the people of England that he came as their liberator and not their conqueror.

James II fled abroad. George Jeffreys tried to escape, disguised as a sailor, but was captured and put in the Tower where he suffered agony from the stone in his kidney. He died the following year, aged 43. As for the executioners, Ketch was later to hang Pascha Rose for murder.

14

A REVOLUTION IN FARMING

The late 18th and early 19th centuries were, in Britain, a period of growth that made her for a time the world's leading economic power. These changes are known as the 'industrial revolution', though industry could not have thrived unless commerce and agriculture had done so simultaneously. As a leading agricultural county, Dorset had an important part to play.

Dorset farmers sent large quantities of food to London, and they also produced some of the raw materials of industry, such as hemp, flax, hides, sheepskins and, above all, wool. As the farming communities prospered, their wealthier members bought more and more industrial goods. Further, some of their capital was invested in commerce and industry. Little enough was direct investment, but most people with money now preferred to deposit it in banks, rather than hoard it at home. Banks then placed their funds where they would earn the best income, which might well include some industrial or trading concerns.

All this was possible because of remarkable progress in farming, though there were hardly any new trends. It was rather that the pace of change became much quicker.

Arthur Young thought that 'spirited improvers' should bring the heathland into cultivation, and some did make the attempt. William Frampton of Moreton grubbed out furze, burnt its roots and then ploughed and harrowed the soil. One of his tenants, William White, started with nothing but prospered as the result of 'severe denial and the most exhausting industry'. He had 120 acres, 16 of which he won from the heath. Squatters also made themselves farms on the heath, for the population was growing and people were desperate for land. But reclamation was only possible where the land was relatively fertile. As always, the heath proper yielded little more than turf and furze for fuel, while the only livestock were a few starving, diseased sheep. Even rabbits did not thrive.

In the vale, some of the clays were improved. One method was to dress them with chalk, which was not too expensive in areas close to the downs. Another method was drainage, to remove surplus water from fields. The result was less evaporation and so less cooling of the soil, resulting in a longer growing season. Drainage was a serious undertaking. There were, as yet, no mass produced earthenware pipes, so ditches two feet deep were filled to within six inches of the surface with stones. Even with all this expense and effort, much of the clay remained intractable. On the lighter soils of Dorset, two horses would plough an acre a day, with one plough. On the heaviest of the clays, though, two teams of four might manage no more than half an acre.

Cultivating the clays and the heath was not good farming, but during the Napoleonic Wars there was a run of bad harvests which made wheat exceptionally dear. Even growing it on unsuitable soils was profitable, and some farmers could not resist the temptation. Then, starting just before the end of the war, there was a run of good harvests. East Anglian farmers met the fall in prices by increasing output, and their wheat came flooding through the Dorset ports. The Dorset farmers, who could not compete, were soon losing up to £2 for every acre of cereals. William Ilott of Milton Abbas lamented, 'It has dwelt a great deal on my mind to see my capital sinking and my family increasing.'

The best answer for the farmers on the clay soils was to use their land in the traditional way, namely for pasturing cattle to supply London with butter and meat. Dorset farmers did not develop their own breed of cattle, which might suggest a lack of enterprise.

In the chalk areas, the most important development was a great increase in the floating of water meadows. Here, Dorset farmers were the leaders. The method has been described in a previous chapter. Its disadvantage was that it took a great deal of time and care and many farmers gave it up when cheap, artificial fertilisers became available towards the end of the 19th century.

Sheep rearing was still the most important activity on the chalk. Early in the 18th century, Daniel Defoe said there were 600,000 sheep within six miles of Dorchester and about a hundred years later, Arthur Young reported flocks as large as 13,000. Young's figure is probably inflated and Defoe's certainly is. Even if every acre were devoted to sheep, an area with a six mile radius would have supported 300,000 at the most. None the less, it is certain that large numbers of sheep were reared in Dorset, and more than that, breeds were much improved.

Nationally, the best known of the 18th century sheep breeders was Robert Bakewell of Leicestershire, but his 'New Leicesters' did not thrive in Dorset. A more promising breed for chalk areas was the Southdown, developed by John Ellman of Glynde in Suffolk, but Dorset farmers

115

had already gone their own way. Their original breed might well have been the one that survived on the Isle of Portland, and if so there was remarkable progress, for the Dorsets of the end of the 18th century weighed three times as much as Portlands and produced twice as much wool. The one advantage the Portlands had, and which explains why they survived, was their excellent mutton. George III greatly appreciated it.

As far as their wool was concerned, the Dorsets were not a success when compared with the Southdowns. An acre of land would support three Dorsets producing, between them, 9¾lbs of wool worth, in 1812, 16s 3d. The same land would support four Southdowns producing eleven pounds of wool worth £1 13s 0d, or over twice the value. Much of the Dorset wool went to a factory at Ilminster, where it was made into livery cloth for uniforms. The Dorsets, though, did give better quality mutton than Southdowns, while their ewes were 'famous twinners'. Cross breeding Dorsets and Southdowns often gave good results.

As in previous centuries, many of the sheep were driven to pastures near London where they were fattened for Smithfield. Some ewes made the journey in lamb and their offspring were suckled in houses for Christmas. This was known as 'house lamb'. Others were fattened on grass to be sold later as 'grass lamb'.

There was progress in arable farming, both on the chalk and in the vale. 'Up and down husbandry' alternated grass and cereals with excellent results, and this was refined with the introduction of new crops. Chief among them was turnips, which Dorset folk at first viewed with suspicion. The Earl of Shaftesbury's steward said that farmers declared 'they could not live by turnips', but, gradually, they became popular. One enterprising gentleman grew some turnips and then gave them, free of charge, to his tenants, 'so that they could ascertain their value.' Formerly, grass seeds had been far too often the sweepings from the hay loft, but now care was taken to buy the best varieties and make the best mixtures. Shaw of Spetisbury sowed 'mixed seeds, consisting of 8lb of broad clover, 4lb of Dutch, half a bushel of Devonshire rye-grass, and sometimes a little hop-clover.' Other fodder crops included tares, rape and sanfoin, as well as the traditional peas and beans. There was now so much winter feed that it was no longer necessary to slaughter any stock in the autumn.

The variety of crops meant a variety of rotations, the standard one being the 'Norfolk four course', which was wheat, turnips, barley or oats and grasses. Some Dorset farmers adhered to this, but it soon exhausted all but the most fertile soils and men experimented to see what suited their own farms best. The simplest variation was to keep the land in

Lime kiln near Abbotsbury. Fuel and chalk were fed from above and the 'burnt' lime was raked out from below. Spread on acid clays it made them 'sweeter' and easier to work. It was an alternative to ground chalk.

grass for a further year or two, but White of Milton Abbas followed an eight course rotation of turnips, oats, beans and vetches, wheat, turnips, oats, clover, wheat. The basic idea was never to grow straw crops for two years following on the same land. However, White reported, 'A few bad farmers must be excepted, who follow a system of their own, consisting of turnips never hoed and several white corn crops taken in succession, which is never the case with the best informed men, and many well-informed men are to be found in every part of the county.'

Another innovation was the use of machinery, especially threshing machines. One owned by Bridge of Wynford Eagle was worked by six oxen, who plodded round in a circle at no more than one and a half miles an hour. But two systems of gears meant that the drum holding the beaters turned 241 times a minute and the beaters themselves had a velocity of 2,410 feet a minute. In eight hours, this machine would thresh 80 bushels of wheat, or 150 bushels of barley, or 180 bushels of oats. Formerly, men had spent the winter threshing the crop with flails, but now the work was finished in a few days.

The enclosure of the wastes, commons and open fields had been going on for centuries. This movement became much more rapid after about 1790, so that within a few decades almost all land that was worth farming had been enclosed. The reason was that the need to enclose became more urgent. The traditional open village had three fields and followed a rotation of wheat, fodder crops and fallow. But fallowing had become unnecessary, while progressive farmers wanted to try rotations of anything up to eight years, which was impossible on three fields. Whole villages could and sometimes did agree to radical improvements, but quite often a group of diehards would prevent progress, so the only answer for the enterprising man was to have his land separate from that of his fellows.

The fact that enclosures made better farming possible was reflected in land values. When Beaminster common was enclosed in 1807, the humble folk who had enjoyed rights to graze their beasts were given half an acre each. Many sold their plots, some for as much as £20. While the common rights had once been let for half-a-crown a year, the rent for an acre of ground was now as high as £5.

With such incentives, landlords and progressive men were unwilling to let cautious or obstructive neighbours stand in their way and they had a remedy, which was to ask Parliament for an enclosure act. The procedures for an act were complicated and, since they involved lawyers and MPs, hideously expensive but, none the less, the gains might be considerable. The act for the Beaminster common cost £1,400, or £2 an acre, but the enclosed land was, as we have seen, worth £5 a year.

The amount of land enclosed at this period varied from village to village. Such cultivated land as there was on the heath had never been held in common, but there were vast tracts of waste. Much of this remained, though there was an enclosure act for Poole, which shared its heath between the burgesses, the town and the lord of the manor. This was worth doing, if only because it ended centuries of wrangling. The Canford and Christchurch acts reserved 425 acres for rough grazing and turf cutting, which had a pleasant result, since the land later became Meyrick, Queen's and King's Parks in Bournemouth. In the vale, many fields had been enclosed from the start, while both here and on the downs there was much enclosure by consent over the centuries. At Sandford Orcas, all that remained by 1804 was a common of 26 acres, which the villagers enclosed by consent. On the other hand, at Kingston Lacy no less than 3,000 acres were still open in 1786, and they were enclosed by Act of Parliament. In the county as a whole, the total amount of land enclosed at this time must have been considerable. Of the 260 parishes, 30 had acts which affected large areas of common arable, while the open downland vanished, as did most of the woods in the vale.

The engrossing of farms went hand in hand with enclosure. The new farming methods needed men of capital, while landowners were happier to deal with a few prosperous tenants rather than large numbers of small men of varying fortunes. At Stourton Caundle in 1709, for example, there were 35 tenants farming, between them, over 250 parcels of land. In 1797 there were nine tenants and 175 fields. Reporting to the Board of Agriculture in 1812, William Stevenson said, 'In many parts of Dorsetshire, one man occupies a whole hamlet, parish or lordship, perhaps from one thousand, or fifteen hundred, or two thousand acres, which has been frequently made by laying five or six farms together.' Most of these very large holdings were on the chalk, since they were especially suitable for sheep.

There were changes, too, in land tenure. Copyhold, which had replaced villeinage, now all but vanished, leaving only freehold and leasehold. Leasehold itself was modified. Once, the lease for 'three lives' had been common. When he took up his lease, the tenant nominated three people and he held his farm until the last of them died. With land values rising rapidly, landowners would not tolerate such a lottery, but wanted to increased rents as often as possible. However, they could not be too greedy, since a tenant would not invest much in his farm unless he was sure he would hold it for a reasonable time. The seven year lease, which was a sound compromise, became quite usual. Further, a good tenant could be fairly sure that his lease would be renewed, though perhaps at a higher rent.

Many humble folk had reason to dislike the changes in farming, but one of the most determined opponents was Baron Rivers, who, as Lord of Cranborne Chase, had the exclusive right to hunt over a quarter of a million acres of Dorset. Chase landowners could not fell trees and could not enclose, nor could they kill any deer, however much damage they might be causing. Turnips were an important new crop, but it was a waste of time to grow them on the Chase, because the deer would be sure to eat them.

There had always been tension between the Lord of the Chase and the landowners, but this increased because of the farming improvements of the late 18th century. The Lord of the Chase was now depriving the landowners of considerable profits. Negotiations began in 1789. Logic was against Rivers, since he hardly needed the deer for food and if it was hunting he wanted, foxes would do perfectly well. The law, though, was on his side and he refused to budge. The second Baron Rivers succeeded his father in 1803, but he was just as intransigent.

The landowners saw the deer as their main enemies, but they felt their best tactic was to try and demonstrate that the Chase laws encouraged crime. There was some truth in this, for the deer attracted poachers, many of whom worked in vicious gangs, and the poachers in turn collaborated with smugglers. There were bloody affrays between poachers and keepers, while in 1779 a band of smugglers routed a detachment of dragoons who had tried to ambush them. The soldiers fled, leaving behind their weapons and their horses.

The bickering went on for 40 years but finally, in 1829, Parliament abolished the Chase laws. The landowners at once slaughtered hundreds of deer.

15

INDUSTRY AND TRANSPORT

During the industrial revolution, none of Dorset's industries could match the success of, for example, Lancashire cotton, and similarly, in transport, the county was hardly a leader. None the less, there were developments of some significance.

Extractive industries prospered. Demand for Portland stone increased as improved communications meant it could be carried further and further afield. The expansion of ball clay mining in the Isle of Purbeck was even more rapid, so that by the 1790s 10,000 tons were going annually to Josiah Wedgwood and other manufacturers in the Staffordshire potteries. Ball clay was a bonding agent in their porcelain, which would have fallen to pieces without it.

Dorset had a variety of handicraft industries, like glove making in the north of the county, silk throwing at Sherborne and lace making at Blandford. This last was brought to the town by Huguenot refugees who fled from France when Louis XIV ended their religious freedom by revoking the Edict of Nantes in 1685. However, the most important industries were button making in east Dorset and rope and net making which were centred on Bridport.

As we have seen, Abraham Case introduced button making to Dorset in 1622. The industry thrived from the start and was boosted in the eighteenth century, partly because there was a useful invention, partly because it was better organised.

Case's buttons were made from slices of sheep horns, covered with fabric and embroidered. But even in Dorset there was a limit to the number of sheep horns, so a bottle neck was created. This was removed early in the eighteenth century by Abraham's grandson, who found that brass wire rings were a good alternative to horn discs. To make the rings, a length of wire was heated, and wound round a rod so that it was the shape of a spring. This was cut along its length, so that it fell apart as a multitude of rings. Their ends were joined by dipping them in molten solder. Finally, the rings were strung together, a gross at a time.

Dorset buttons. These are 'cross wheels'. They are mounted on yellow card, so they are seconds.

The children who did the work were known as 'winders', 'dippers' and 'stringers'. The winders risked burns, and the dippers both burns and lead poisoning.

The reorganisation of the industry was largely the work of John Clayton, who began working for the Cases in 1731. He made the existing system of 'putting out' more efficient. There were two central depots, one at Shaftesbury and another at Bere Regis, where the wire rings were made and where linen and thread were stored. There were also some well scattered minor depots, usually rooms in pubs, at such places as Wool, Sixpenny Handley, Piddletrenthide and Langton Matravers. Every week, on 'button day', the workers came to these depots, where they met Case's agents and exchanged their finished buttons for their wages and more materials. The buttons then went back to the central depots, where they were sorted and put on cards, pink for 'superior' buttons, blue for 'standards' and yellow for 'seconds'.

As well as these improvements, many more types of button were made. By the end of the 18th century there were no less than a hundred, including high-tops, honeycombs, crosswheels, singletons, yannells, birds-eyes, old Dorsets, mites, spangles, Blandford cartwheels and Dorset knobs. Mites and spangles were very small buttons; high tops were used for hunting waistcoats; Blandford cartwheels had been developed by the Huguenot refugees, for use with their lace.

Only women and children worked at button making. The younger children did the 'casting', which was covering the rings with thread, while the older girls and the women did the 'filling', or embroidery. A skilled woman could make up to a gross of buttons a day and earn herself twelve shillings a week. If her husband was a farm worker, he might have earned no more than eight shillings.

It is impossible to say how many people worked at buttony, but Case alone employed 700 in 1730 and 4,000 in 1803. Another firm, Atchinsons, was employing 1,200 in 1793. There was a similar increase in turnover; Case's was £9,000 in 1766 and £14,000 in 1807.

The main reason for the growth of the Dorset industry was the expansion of the cotton manufacture in Lancashire. With the northern mills turning out cloth by the mile, buttons were needed in their tens of thousands. The Cases had offices in both London and Liverpool, which handled exports that went all over Europe and North America. Peter Case, who inherited the firm in 1758, showed his gratitude to Liverpool by building Case's Street and Clayton Square in the city.

Due to government interference and guild restrictions, the Bridport rope and net industries had stagnated in the 16th and 17th centuries. There were further problems in the early 18th century. Some of the more enterprising Bridport men left to carry on their trade in places as far away as Yorkshire. The Navy decided it would no longer buy its heavy cables from Bridport, since the largest were now 25 inches in circumference and difficult to transport. The harbour at West Bay was, as usual, full of silt. However, prosperity returned after about 1740, due to an increase in the numbers of fishing vessels and merchant ships and hence a greater demand for ropes and nets. The harbour was dredged and its piers rebuilt, which, apart from helping industry in the town, encouraged shipbuilding. The roads were turnpiked, making it easier for merchants to use other local ports like Poole and Lyme Regis.

As well as making ropes, the Bridport manufacturers also spun string, pack-thread and twine. From 1750 there was a new industry, sail making. The best place to make sails, it was thought, was West Coker in Somerset, due to some quality in the water, so Bridport manufacturers described their sails as 'made at Bridport near Coker' and relied on their customers' ignorance of geography. However, it was net making that became the main occupation, chiefly fishing nets of all kinds. Bridport folk gave their nets names, like Lance, Caplin and Dongarbin and even had a special Bridport knot for making them.

Most ropes and nets were still sold in Newfoundland. The fisheries

Eighteenth century rope and net factory, Bridport.

reached a peak during the Napoleonic Wars when the Royal Navy blockaded the European ports, and as Newfoundland prospered, so did Bridport. For a sideline, the ships carried Madeira wine, which makes better drinking after a long sea voyage. It was best to send it round the world, but four return trips to Newfoundland were nearly as good.

There were changes in the organisation of the industries. By tradition rope making was a family business, but in the 18th century capitalists took charge. They came from the ranks of the middle men who, since the 16th century, had been buying hemp and flax from farmers and selling to manufacturers. Samuel Gundry was 'putting out' work as early as 1685. The manufacturer no longer bought his hemp, but made up what Gundry gave him, so he was paid only for his labour and the use of his equipment. Instead of being independent, he had become Gundry's employee. However, he no longer had to buy his raw materials and he was spared the worry of marketing his goods. The change was probably good for the industry as a whole, because the capitalists, with their longer purses, were better able to cope with the trade depressions that occurred every few years. Net making was run in the same way, the employers putting out twine and the cottagers working at home.

The old guild restrictions went. How or why is not clear, but the result was that instead of having a stagnant industry in Bridport, and a barren no man's land five miles wide, the countryside for ten miles around was busy, while the town hummed with life.

Here was an industrial revolution in miniature, and it took place without any new inventions. The technology remained simple. The flax and hemp leaves were 'retted', or steeped in water, so that the green matter decomposed, releasing the fibres. These were 'scutched', which meant beating them to knock out the seeds, and they were then combed. The flax was spun on a wheel, like the kind used for wool or cotton, but rope making was done in walks, which were long, narrow enclosures. Here, two people worked; a child, known as a turner and a man who was the spinner. The turner stood at a wheel with a hook in the middle that held the combed hemp, while the spinner drew out the hemp as it was twisted, walking slowly backwards. He went up and back 160 yards, four times in an hour, perhaps for ten hours a day. If he had a working life of 50 years, he walked the equivalent of three times round the world. Some of the turners were parish apprentices who had only their board and lodging, though some were 'free' children who earned up to two shillings a week.

Net making was women's work. It was ideal for a domestic craft, since the goods were easy to transport and the equipment simple, just a wooden needle and some hooks on the wall. Whenever possible, the women worked outside. As they did little more than tie knots they must have been bored, but they did not look for variety, since each village specialised in its own kind of net and refused to change.

The industrial revolution is usually associated with 'dark, satanic mills', and their evil reputation for exploiting children. Dorset had few mills, none of them large. There were silk throwing mills at Sherborne and Gillingham, while Bourton had a water powered mill for spinning flax. There was also Grove Mill at Burton Bradstock, built by Richard Roberts for scutching flax. Roberts's favourite workers were little girls aged from eight to ten, because, he said, they were the most obedient. Most of them lived near the mill, but to make up his numbers he took orphans from workhouses as far afield as Ottery St Mary, Cranborne and Shepton Mallett. Roberts assured the overseers that the children would be 'taken as good care of, or perhaps better than at home, both for food and raiment and morals, and will not have hard work to do more than twelve hours a day.'

The fact that Dorset had few mills does not mean that there was little exploitation of children in the county. The rope spinners of Bridport made their parish apprentices turn for hours on end. Case employed children as winders, dippers and stringers, and if a woman was to fill a gross of buttons in a day, then her children would first have to cast them

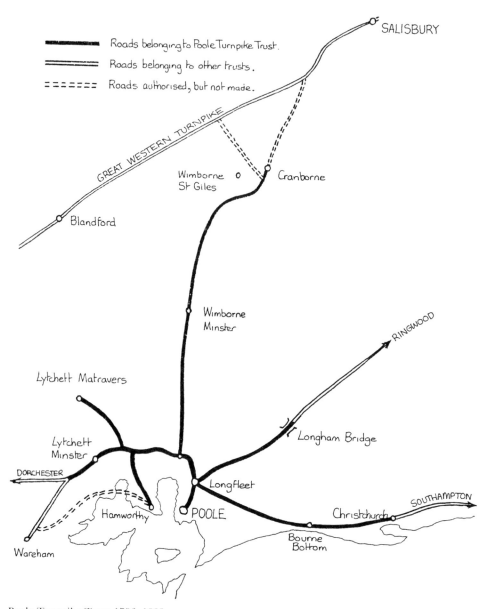

SALISBURY

GREAT WESTERN TURNPIKE

Wimborne
St Giles

Cranborne

Blandford

Wimborne
Minster

RINGWOOD

Lytchett Matravers

Longham Bridge

Lytchett
Minster

DORCHESTER

Longfleet

SOUTHAMPTON

Hamworthy

POOLE

Christchurch

Wareham

Bourne
Bottom

Poole Turnpike Trust 1756–1882.

for her. Children did the simpler tasks, but they were also the dullest, and only savage discipline would have kept them working. As for the homes where the children toiled, the Medical Officer of the Cerne Abbas Poor Law Union wrote:

> Most of the cottages are of the worst kind; some are mud hovels with cesspools or piles of filth close to the doors. The mud floors of

Crawford Bridge, Spetisbury. Bridges were as essential as roads. This one is medieval on the far side, while the near side is of 1819, though with a reset datestone of 1719.

many are much below the level of the road and in wet seasons are little better than so much clay. I have often seen springs bursting through the mud floors of some of the cottages, and little channels cut from the centre under the doorways to carry off the water, whilst the door had been removed from its hinges for the children to put their feet on whilst making buttons.

Neither farming nor industry could have made much progress without good roads. The Romans had built an excellent network, but it was neglected after the collapse of the empire. From Saxon times onwards, most roads were just tracks which farmers used to go to and from their fields. Road improvement began in the 18th century with the formation of turnpike trusts. A group of local dignitaries, such as landowners, merchants and manufacturers, would form a trust and then apply to Parliament for an act which would allow them to improve the roads in their neighbourhood. They recouped their expenses by putting up gates and levying tolls.

The Poole, Wimborne and Cranborne Trust will serve as an example for Dorset. It obtained its act in 1756, whereby it was given charge of the roads shown on the map. There was a spur to Lytchett Matravers because, in the early days, the main road to Bere Regis and Dorchester went that way. The Trust abandoned this spur when a more direct road to Dorchester was opened. In 1818 another act allowed the Trust to make the two links with the Great Western Turnpike. Most of the roads were existing ones which the Trust improved, but there was a new stretch most of the way between Poole and Wimborne. At its peak, the Trust maintained, or was supposed to maintain, 43½ miles of roads.

The Poole Trust, like most of its kind, showed great respect to landowners. The road from Wimborne to Cranborne curves politely round the boundary of the Earl of Shaftesbury's park at Wimborne St Giles. The Trust even changed the line of its road at Upton so that Christopher Spurrier could make a park for Upton House. Neither bend, though, could match the loop which the Blandford to Shaftesbury turnpike made round Stapleton House. The modern road still follows the same line.

In 1836, an Act of Parliament authorised some contraction of the Poole Trust. The spur to Lytchett Matravers was abandoned, presumably because there was now a more direct road to Bere Regis further south. The Trust also gave up the links between Cranborne and the Great West Turnpike. Indeed, these had never been made. Today, Cranborne looks like a village that should have become a town, but failed to do so. It did not generate enough traffic to justify new roads, so it remained the dead end of a turnpike, while the main route bypassed it.

There were trusts similar to Poole's all over England. They spread their tentacles and while some, like the Cranborne road, went into the void or withered at the ends, most of them joined others. Eventually, there was a national road system that had been created without any central planning at all. From Dorchester, for example, there were through roads leading to Weymouth, Southampton, Bristol and Bath, and the town was also on the Great Western Turnpike which led from London to Salisbury and then to Exeter and Plymouth.

Turnpike trusts employed professional surveyors, so that the quality of roads improved. This led to better coaches, which were lighter and faster. The time from Sherborne to London, for example, was cut from two days to twelve hours. There were plenty of coaches. The following ran from Blandford in 1825:

Daily – London:	7.45 am, 12.45 and 5.00 pm.
Weymouth:	5.00 am and 6.00 pm.
Exeter:	5.30 am and 9.00 am.
Three times a week –	Brighton, via Southampton and Portsmouth.
	Exeter, in addition to above.
	Bath and Bristol.
	Poole.

An unusual service used light carts, drawn by relays of Newfoundland dogs, to take fresh plaice from Poole to London.

Coach travel was not for ordinary folk. It would have taken a Dorset farm labourer three weeks to earn the fare from Blandford to London, even riding outside. In the unlikely event of such a man wanting to make the journey, he would have walked or travelled in a goods waggon.

The late 18th and early 19th centuries were the great age of canals, and in 1793 one was suggested which would have run from Bath and Bristol, through Blandford, and on to Poole. The Bristol and English Channels would have been linked, avoiding the long, dangerous voyage round Lands End. The plan sounded exciting but was too ambitious. Later, there was a more modest proposal for a canal which would have ended at Shillingston, just to the north-west of Blandford. There was to be a spur leading from near Frome to the North Somerset coalfield, and the chief value of the canal might have been to bring coal into Dorset. However, only part of the spur was completed and work on the main canal never even began. Dorset remained one of the few English counties to have no canals at all.

16

TRADERS AND SMUGGLERS

None of Dorset's ports could compare with Bristol, Liverpool or Glasgow, and still less, London. Further, Dorset merchants played little or no part in the highly profitable slave trade. But while the county's trade contributed only a little to the wealth of Britain as a whole, it did, for a time, benefit an important minority of local people.

Poole's Newfoundland trade continued to prosper. In the 17th century, London and Bristol tried to secure a monopoly in Newfoundland, but they were frustrated by the so-called 'Western Charters' which guaranteed the rights of West Country ports. Eventually, Poole's only serious rival was Dartmouth. The French were also banished, for they lost their rights in Newfoundland by the Treaty of Utrecht, which ended the War of the Spanish Succession in 1713.

In the early days, only a dozen or so Poole ships sailed to Newfoundland each year. By the 1720s some 40 ships took part in the trade, and this increased to more than 70 in the 1770s. Then came the Napoleonic Wars. From time to time the press gang descended on Poole to take sailors for the navy, but there were enormous compensations. After gaining control of the seas at Trafalgar in 1805, the Royal Navy blockaded the European ports. Further, in 1808, Wellington's army came to the aid of Spain and Portugal, who, as a result, allowed the British to trade with themselves and their colonies on favourable terms. From then until the war ended in 1815, up to 350 Poole vessels went to Newfoundland every year.

In Newfoundland there were many emigrants from Dorset, including some orphans from the workhouse at Wimborne, and numbers were made up by people from Ireland. These settlers treated the fish. 'Headers' removed both heads and tails, 'splitters' boned and gutted the fish, and 'spreaders' salted them before laying them on brushwood 'flakes' to dry. The livers were thrown into barrels, where they dissolved into 'train oil'. This was a disgusting liquid, but it was in demand for lamps and was also used for preparing wool, tanning leather and making soap. Poole stank of it.

Most of the goods needed in Newfoundland were exported, or re-exported, from Poole. Foodstuffs included grain, flour, oatmeal, biscuits, peas, salt meat, cider, beer, tea and brandy. Fresh foods such as cheese, butter and vegetables were picked up in southern Ireland. Manufactured goods included hats, gloves, handkerchiefs, shoes, crockery, glassware, furniture, bricks, musical instruments, grindstones, gunpowder, tobacco and pipes. Most important of all were the items needed in the fishing industry, such as salt, ropes, chains, sails, blocks, nets and lines.

Certain of Newfoundland's products came to Dorset, including train oil, seal pelts, furs, cranberries and timber, especially staves for making casks. At one time it was thought that the pinewood columns in St James's church had been towed across the Atlantic, though it is more likely that they came from Riga in one of the great Baltic timber ships. But Newfoundland's staple product was dried cod, for which there was little demand in England. It went elsewhere. By the 18th century there were many slaves in the West Indies whose owners were happy to feed them on dried cod, which, though unappetising, was cheap and nourishing. Vessels going to the West Indies brought home rum and molasses. Most of the fish, though, went as it always had done to Spain, Portugal and Italy, where there were large numbers of poor Roman Catholics. From here, the imports were citrus fruits, dried fruits and wine.

The Newfoundland trade brought prosperity both to Poole and its hinterland. Shipyards were busy, repairing and building vessels. In the town, butchers slaughtered whole herds of cattle and salted the beef. There was also work for tanners, shoemakers, blockmakers, carpenters, blacksmiths and many others. Swanskin flannel came from Sturminster Newton and linen from Lytchett, while Bridport supplied sails, ropes, nets and lines.

Though many humble folk thrived, the people who made most from the Newfoundland trade were the merchants. When John Slade died in 1792, he left £70,000. Joseph White had an estate in Newfoundland employing 200 people and a fleet of twelve fishing boats and ten sailing vessels. When he died in 1771 he was worth £150,000. Benjamin Lester had twelve ships in the 1770s and 30 by the 1790s, probably the largest fleet of all. In typical merchant fashion, these men flaunted their wealth by building expensive houses. Much of this marvellous heritage has been lost, but we still have, for example, the Slades' Poole House, Benjamin Lester's Mansion House, and Beech Hurst, built for Joseph White's heir, Samuel Rolles. The most ambitions of the merchants was probably Christopher Spurrier, who bought a seat in Parliament and, in 1816, built Upton House, set in a park of 900 acres.

The ending of the Napoleonic Wars was a disaster for Dorset's

Newfoundland trade. The price of fish fell from 40 shillings a quintal to twelve shillings, so Poole merchants could no longer make a profit. It was Christopher Spurrier's misfortune that he built Upton House just as the slump was beginning and, in view of his extravagance, few were surprised when he went bankrupt. Soon, though, responsible men were failing and by the 1840s the trade was as good as dead.

Writing in 1839, Poole's historian John Sydenham blamed foreigners. Spain and Portugal were protecting their own fisheries with duties and their people had changed their eating habits; the Norwegians had entered the market; the French and the Americans were allowed on the Grand Banks. Moreover, in Newfoundland itself, there was 'insecurity of property owing to the wide spreading of popish influence among the labouring classes.'

There was another problem which Sydenham does not mention. The marvellous houses in Poole are indeed evidence of merchant prosperity, but they are evidence, too, of an extravagant life style. This must have been financed with money which would have been better invested in businesses. Poole's merchants prospered when the Royal Navy was sweeping their rivals from the seas, but they were unprepared for competition and collapsed when it came.

Piracy was suppressed in the reign of Elizabeth I, but there was still good money to be made from smuggling. Governments put heavy duties on certain imports, partly to control trade and partly to raise revenue. A keg of brandy, for example, cost the equivalent of 16 shillings in France and, duty paid, 32 shillings in England. Smuggled, it cost only 22 shillings.

Smugglers concentrated on goods that were valuable in relation to their weight, such as spirits, tea, coffee, silk and lace. A favourite landing place was Poole Bay, for there were hardly any settlements, the chines made convenient gaps in the cliffs and inland was an empty heath. Canford Cliffs road in Poole, now a broad highway lined with expensive houses, was once a dusty track leading from Flaghead Chine and called Smugglers' Way.

Smuggling needed capital, so any trip would be organised by someone with money, like a landowner. He was known as the 'venturer' and it was he who hired the smuggling vessel and her crew. Bringing the goods ashore was the responsibility of the 'lander', who recruited labourers and encouraged farmers to leave their stable doors open. 'Batmen' protected the convoys. They armed themselves with clubs, since resisting the revenue officers with firearms carried the death penalty.

Much smuggling was done at night and in secret, but not all of it. The

West End House, ca. 1716, home of a Newfoundland merchant.

Rev Richard Warner of Christchurch, writing of the 1770s, said that he had, 'more than once seen a procession of twenty or thirty waggons loaded with kegs of spirits, an armed man at the front and tail of each and surrounded by a troop of two or three hundred horsemen, each carrying on his enormous saddle from two to four tubs of spirits, winding deliberately and with the most picturesque and imposing effect along the skirts of Hengistbury Head on their way to the wild country to the north-east of Christchurch.'

Inland, the horsemen dispersed and took their goods to various hiding places. One such was Kinson church, where the parapet of the tower still has grooves worn by ropes that were used to haul up contraband.

In 1698 the government established the Preventive Service and riding officers were appointed. Pay was low and an officer had to provide his own horse, but there were plenty of recruits, perhaps because of the chance of prize money and the opportunity to make deals with smugglers. In 1713 detachments of dragoons were stationed along the coast. They were mounted infantry, who rode to the place of action and then fought on foot, exactly the tactics needed to deal with smugglers. From 1759 navy cutters were also helping. The service was reorganised in the early 19th century, coastguards and revenue cutters replacing the riding officers and the armed forces.

It was difficult to control the smugglers for various reasons. There was a certain amount of corruption. In 1681 it emerged that the most powerful of the Poole smugglers were a merchant called John Carter and his partner Moses Durell. Carter was a magistrate, and both men had been mayors. In 1759 the Poole Supervisor of Excise claimed, while drunk and therefore more likely to tell the truth, that the customs officers of the town were 'very considerable smugglers'. Like piracy in earlier centuries, smuggling carried no moral stigma. Indeed, smugglers were seen as friends of the people, since they supplied duty free goods. When the vicar of Christchurch was rash enough to declare smuggling a sin, his clerk replied, 'Then may the Lord have mercy on the poor town of Christchurch, your Reverence, for who is there here that has not had a tub?' At Kinson, the tombstone of a smuggler shot by revenue men has an inscription which shows the popular attitude:

A little Tea one leaf I did not steal.
For Guiltless Blood shed, I to GOD appeal.
Put Tea in one scale human Blood in tother
And think what tis to slay thy harmless Brother.

Further, it was unwise for a revenue officer to be too zealous in his duties. After one Bursey had been making a nuisance of himself, two smugglers lured him to his door and beat out his brains.

Yet another problem was that a gang of smugglers landing could be like an army of invasion which only a large body of troops would dare to attack. There were some lively affrays, including the so-called Battle of Mudeford of 1784. Joshua Jeans, the Supervisor of Riding Officers of Christchurch, heard that a convoy of waggons was making its way to the coast, obviously intending to pick up contraband. Jeans advised his men to follow his example and go home to bed, so all might have passed off peacefully had not Captain Ellis of HMS *Orestes* spotted the smugglers unloading. He manned six boats and ordered one of his officers, William Allen, to lead an attack. The smugglers retreated to the Haven Inn where they beat off the navy men and killed Allen.

During the middle years of the 18th century there was a band of smugglers that operated, for the most part, in Kent and Sussex. It was known as the Hawkhurst Gang, since it was based on the Kentish village of that name. In 1747 one of the gang's vessels was captured and its cargo was lodged in the customs house at Poole. When the smugglers heard of this, 30 of them entered the town, smashed the doors of the customs house and made off with close on two tons of tea, 40 barrels of spirits and a large bag of coffee. All of it was their own property; they

Ships off Poole quay, 1833 (Poole Museums Service).

touched nothing that belonged to anyone else. This was in line with their policy of keeping on friendly terms with the general public and was no proof that they were good fellows at heart, as is shown in the sequel.

When the smugglers were passing through Fordingbridge, one of them, John Diamond, saw an old acquaintance called Daniel Chater and tossed him a bag of tea. Soon afterwards, Diamond was captured and locked in Chichester gaol. Moreover, the incident of the bag of tea was reported to the authorities who despatched an elderly revenue man, William Galley, to fetch Chater, hoping that he might identify Diamond and even make a statement. While on the journey, Chater let slip its purpose while he and Galley were at an inn, whereupon some smugglers took both men prisoner. After torturing them, they buried Galley alive and flung Chater down a well.

Dorset's most famous smuggler was Isaac Gulliver, known as the 'gentleman smuggler' because in all his long career no one was killed as a result of his activities, or so he claimed. Gulliver organised well. He had a band of between 40 and 50 highly trained, liveried servants known from their coiffure as the 'White Wigs'; he had a sophisticated system of warning lights; he planted a clump of trees on Eggardon Hill to act as a marker for his vessels; his house at Kinson had an underground passage and a secret room with its only door ten feet up the inside of a chimney. Gulliver was also clever at avoiding capture. Perhaps his most daring escapade was to whiten his face with hair powder and lie in a coffin, pretending to be dead. The officer who came to arrest him withdrew, shamefaced and apologetic.

Eventually, Gulliver accepted a royal pardon. The story was that he uncovered a plot against George III and the king is reputed to have said, 'Let Gulliver smuggle as much as he likes.' It is more probable that Gulliver took advantage of a general pardon of 1782 offered to smugglers who would join the navy, or find two substitutes instead. He then settled in Wimborne as an honest dealer in wine, spirits and tea, though his prices were so competitive that his goods must have been duty free. Gulliver was well respected in Wimborne. One of his daughters married a doctor and another a banker, while he himself became a churchwarden. When he died, he was buried in the Minster.

Smuggling became more difficult in the 1830s when coastguards were better trained and magistrates more severe, but the end came during the following decade, when government policy changed from protection to free trade. On taking office in 1841, Robert Peel found that 1,046 articles were liable to duty. By degrees, he abolished it entirely on 605 of them and drastically reduced it on the remainder.

Another illegal activity connected with the sea was the plundering of wrecks. The Dorset coast is dangerous, especially so because of the Isle of Portland. If a vessel was driven into Lyme Bay by a south-westerly gale, she would quite likely be unable to round the Bill and would end up on Chesil Beach. Many ships were lost over the centuries, including six military transports that foundered in 1795 with the loss of 234 lives.

News of a wreck brought out the crowds. When a vessel was in difficulties in 1838, part of Chesil Beach was, according to a customs officer, 'completely lined with men, women and children whose only object was plunder.' The greatest prize seems to have been the *Hope of Amsterdam*. She had taken a valuable cargo to South America and in January 1748 she was returning with, among other things, gold dust, silver and jewels. One foggy night she was driven on to Chesil Beach. The crew landed safely, but the ship herself was at the mercy of the mobs that flocked in from miles around. The men of Portland, Weymouth and Wyke Regis were particularly well organised under their own colours, in teams of 20. It was days before the justices of the peace could muster enough armed men to disperse the crowd.

There is no proof that Dorset folk deliberately caused wrecks, as the Cornish did, and it is calumnious to say that the good people of Portland were 'always praying for wrecks.' Their supplication was, in fact, 'We do not pray, Lord, that wrecks should happen, but if wrecks must happen, then let them happen here.'

17

HIGH LIFE AND LOW LIFE

The leaders of Dorset society were the landowners. Some were eccentrics and wastrels, but most of them were serious minded. It was they who obtained the enclosure acts and engrossed the farms, so making possible the revolution in agriculture. The hedgerows that cover the countryside are their most important legacy, but that was not all they left by any means.

The 18th century was one of the golden ages of English architecture, for building was in the classical tradition. Dorset has some fine houses of the period. Chettle is, in Pevsner's words, 'the plum among Dorset houses of the early 18th century, and even nationally outstanding as a specimen of English Baroque.' The architect Thomas Archer built it for George Chafin, a ranger of Cranborne Chase, in about 1715. The walls are of brick, with dressings of Chilmark stone. The giant pilasters are capped with strangely grooved capitals, for Baroque architects did not adhere too strictly to classical forms. The wings have rounded ends, which is pleasantly unusual. Originally, they were only of one and a half storeys, but the Victorians added a storey, making them nearly as high as the central block. Inside there are some fine rooms, while the entrance hall and staircase are magnificent.

Merley House was built in the 1750s for Ralph Willett, the son of a West Indian sugar planter. Willett claimed that he designed the house himself. The façade, with its huge Ionic columns and triangular pediment, follows the classical rules exactly. The house would have looked even more magnificent when it had its four supporting pavilions, but these were demolished in the 19th century. The house's main attraction today is its splendid ceilings.

Creech Grange is more restrained than Chettle or Merley, but set as it is, deep in the countryside, it is a gem.

The 18th century also saw a new kind of park, which swept right up to the house, with no formal gardens intervening. There is a good example at Melbury Stamford and an even better one at Sherborne Castle, the work of 'Capability' Brown. Something similar, but pleasantly original,

Chettle House.

was the clump of trees that Henry Bankes planted on Badbury Rings in 1741. There were five vistas from the centre of the clump, each framing an important landmark. The magnificent avenue of beeches along the road beside the Rings dates from 1835.

After the dissolution of the monasteries, the church of Milton Abbey became the parish church of Middleton, while the monastery buildings were converted into a home. Then, in 1752, the estate was bought by one Joseph Damer, shortly to become Lord Milton and eventually Earl of Dorchester. Walpole described him as, 'The most arrogant and proud of men, with no foundation but great wealth and a match with the Duke of Dorset's daughter.' Damer disliked having the town so close to his house, and he found its grammar school especially irritating, because the boys robbed his orchard, dropped stones down his chimneys and stole the eggs of his game birds to rear fighting cocks. But Damer had great plans. He would pull down the monastery buildings to make room for a fine, new mansion, he would make the abbey church his own private chapel, and he would move the town well out of his way.

From 1760, Damer was buying the leases of the houses in the town. Many of the inhabitants surrendered without a fuss, but others resisted, including a lawyer called Harrison. Damer had the sluice gates of the abbot's pond opened, flooding Harrison's house. The school was the last

Staircase of Chettle House.

to go, for Damer needed an Act of Parliament to shift it and did not succeed until 1785. It was then moved seven miles away to Blandford. The people of Middleton were given a new village, Milton Abbas, which was tucked round a corner in a valley, out of sight of the house.

Damer instructed his architect, Sir William Chambers, to build a house that would match the church, but devoted as he was to classical architecture, Chambers could not do the work of a medieval master mason. It was against all his instincts. Inevitably, Damer's grandiose plan was an architectural failure. Placed well apart, the house and the church might have formed a pleasing contrast, but side by side as they are, they make an ill-assorted couple.

Dorset's most ambitious building of the 18th century was Eastbury House. It was begun for George Dodington, who had accumulated a fortune in India. Dodington died in 1720, before the house was finished, and his nephew, George Bubb, inherited it along with the fortune. Bubb Dodington, as he now called himself, decided to complete the house in style, and where his uncle had expected it would cost £30,000, spent £140,000. Paul Bridgeman, who had designed Kensington Gardens, laid out the park and the architect was the great Sir John Vanbrugh, famous as the creator of Blenheim Palace. Bubb Dodington

139

Guildhall, Poole, 1761. This was the gift of Joseph Gulston and Thomas Calcraft, the town's MPs.

saw himself as a patron of literature and entertained many luminaries at Eastbury, including Voltaire and Fielding.

Unfortunately, Eastbury was, like Blenheim, 'a house and not a dwelling.' For all its magnificence it was cold and damp, the walls running with condensation. When the Grenville family inherited the place in 1762 they found it a liability. Their first move was to offer £200 a year to anyone who would live in it, and when there were no takers they demolished everything but the stable court.

All of Dorset's towns are graced with at least some 18th century buildings, while nearly the whole of the centres of Blandford, Wareham and Bridport belong to that period. Prosperity is one explanation for this. Bridport's fine buildings reflect the wealth its people made from their markets, from their rope and net industries, and from catering for travellers on the Great Western Turnpike. Poole owes some superb houses to its trade with Newfoundland.

Fires are another explanation. On 4th June 1731, sparks fell into the thatch of a soap-boiler's workshop at Blandford, starting a fire which destroyed much of the town. The church collapsed into the flames, the bells melted and the metal ran down the street. In 1762 there was a blaze which burnt the heart out of Wareham and there were fires at Dorchester in 1725, 1732, 1775, 1779 and 1789. These, though, were the last of the conflagrations that had plagued the towns for centuries, the main reason being that people were building with stone, brick and tile, rather than timber and thatch. Thus, the 18th century saw the destruction of many old buildings and their replacement with others of such quality that they have lasted for over 200 years.

The town houses are in the same excellent taste as the larger country houses and, indeed, some were built by the same people. Dorchester was a favourite resort of the landed gentry, numbers of whom made second homes in the town. There are some superb examples in High West Street. Here, and in other places, merchants and professional men also built in the classical style, usually with the happiest of results. Bridport had a flying start, since East, West and South Streets were already wide to accommodate the markets. Lined as they are with Georgian buildings, these streets are most impressive. Even the humbler houses are well proportioned and pleasing.

During the 18th century, Weymouth and Lyme Regis became seaside resorts. Both towns had been declining, but in the 1750s doctors began recommending sea water as a cure for many ills, especially fashionable ones like gout. Dr Richard Russel, for example, wrote a dissertation on the value of sea water, advising people to bathe in it and even drink it. Ralph Allen was one of those who took the cure and in 1763 he invented the bathing machine. This device, which was a bit like a gypsy caravan, allowed people to strip and enter the water unobserved.

Weymouth, with its mild climate and splendid beach, was an ideal place for bathing. The first person of note to discover this was George III's brother, the Duke of Gloucester, who built himself a house known as Gloucester Lodge, today the Gloucester Hotel. The Duke placed his house on the sea front, which was a new fashion, since in those days many were still doubtful about exposing themselves to the elements.

For example, Gloucester's nephew, the Prince Regent, kept Brighton Pavilion a respectful distance from the beach.

In 1789 the Duke persuaded the king to join him, after which George visited the town nearly every year until 1805. The novelist and diarist Fanney Burney wrote, 'Think but of the surprise of His Majesty when, the first time of his bathing, he had no sooner popped his royal head under water, than a band of music, concealed in a neighbouring machine, struck up "God Save great George our King".' As well as bathing, George III was fond of sea trips. A visitor to Weymouth wrote, 'The king never seemed afraid of the weather. The queen and princesses always wore blue habits on these occasions and I have often seen them look very miserable and bedraggled on their return.'

The people of Weymouth honoured George III by cutting an equestrian figure of him on the hills near Osmington, and by erecting a statue to him to celebrate his golden jubilee. The king saw neither of them, for he paid his last visit to Weymouth in 1805, before they were finished. By then, though, he had made the town a fashionable resort. In the early 19th century splendid terraces were built along the Esplanade and nobles and gentlemen took houses in them as their 'summer residences'.

The transformation of Lyme Regis was begun by the philanthropist, Thomas Holles, who had an estate near Beaminster. He rebuilt houses, constructed a promenade and started an assembly rooms. There were no royal visitors, but in 1772 Holles persuaded his friend William Pitt, Earl of Chatham, to bring his ailing son to Lyme for the sea air. Chatham, one of Britain's greatest prime ministers, was the architect of victory against France in the Seven Years War. His son, another William, was to be prime minister during the wars against revolutionary France and win even more fame than his father.

Holles died in 1774, but his work continued. Lyme's geography did not allow magnificent terraces, but the rich built themselves villas and 'cottages ornés'. They came to Lyme after the Bath season ended in September and stayed until November.

Jane Austen was in Lyme in 1803–1804. She danced in the Assembly Rooms, walked on the Cobb and bathed. Miss Austen wrote to her sister saying, 'The bathing was so delightful and Molly so pressing with me to enjoy myself that I believe I stayed in rather long.' In *Persuasion*, Louisa Musgrove falls from the Cobb, an incident that has greatly endeared Jane Austen to the people of Lyme.

Lyme had a special attraction in Mary Anning (1799–1847), who might be the original lady who 'sold sea shells on the sea shore'. The Jurassic clays in the cliffs near the town are full of fossils, which are constantly

Gloucester Row, The Esplanade, Weymouth. The marvellous wrought iron balconies are typical of the Regency period.

appearing as the clays erode. Mary Anning was only one of the Lyme folk who gathered fossils to sell to visitors, but she was so skilful that she became famous. In spite of her lack of education, she was elected a member of the Royal Society. Her finds included the first complete plesiosaurus and a dimorphodon, a kind of gliding reptile. At the time, many people thought these were the skeletons of creatures that had been refused admission to Noah's Ark.

Like most other coastal resorts, those in Dorset gained from the Romantic Movement, which discovered beauties in nature that had escaped earlier generations. Once, the sea had been the cause of shipwreck and destruction, as well as a highway for pirates, raiders and foreign enemies. Now it was to be admired for its strength and majesty. Just a few reactionaries remained, like the bemused Lulworth fisherman who exclaimed, 'I keep out of the water as much as I can, and I cannot see why you London folk come down here at vast expense to souse and sop yourselves in salt water.'

The wars with France, which dragged on from 1793 to 1815, also helped the resorts, because for most of the time the wealthy could not travel in Europe and had to console themselves at home. Dorset's visitors compared Lyme Bay to the Bay of Naples, with Golden Cap standing in for Vesuvius.

The restoration of the monarchy in 1660 had also meant the restoration of the power and influence of the Church of England, but the Puritan sects survived. Their members became known as Dissenters and, later, as Nonconformists.

During the second half of the 17th century new sects appeared. George Fox founded the Society of Friends in 1650 and, after the Restoration, the Independents divided into Congregationalists and Baptists. A leading Dorset Baptist was William Baily of Poole. He wrote numerous tracts, including *Jacob is become a flame and Esau stubble, A grievous lamentation over thee, O England!* and *An arrow shot against Babylon out of Jacob's bow.*

George Fox came to Dorset several times. His *Journal* describes a visit to Poole in 1655:

> Having set up our horses at an inn, we sent into the town to enquire for such as fear the Lord and who were worthy; and we had a meeting there, with several sober people; and William Baily, a baptist teacher, was convinced there at that time. The people received the truth in the inward parts, and were turned to the Lord Jesus Christ; and there is become a great gathering in the name of Jesus, of a very tender people, who continue under Christ's teaching.

Baily left Poole to spread the Word, which he did with such enthusiasm that he was persecuted. In the end, he was sentenced to transportation to the West Indies and died at sea.

The 18th century saw the appearance of the most important of the new sects, Methodism. John Wesley's grandfather had been the incumbent at Winterborne Whitchurch and was evicted for expressing radical views soon after 1660. Wesley himself made several visits to Dorset, preaching, it would seem, with growing success. When he was at Shaftesbury in 1750, 'one or two foul-mouthed women spoke unseemly' and the mayor tried to stop him preaching. Thirty years later, Wesley was pleased to see the former mayor in his congregation.

Parliament imposed severe restrictions on Dissenters. For example, the Test Act of 1673 stated that only communicant members of the Church of England could hold public office. James II courted the Dissenters, but they refused to support him during the Glorious Revolution of 1688. For this, they were rewarded with the Toleration Act of 1689, which allowed them their own places of worship. They were still debarred from office until the repeal of the Test Act in 1828, though Parliament had for some time been passing annual acts of indemnity.

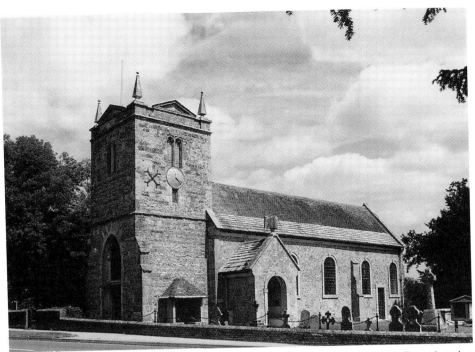

St Mary's, Charlton Marshall, 1713. Church building almost ceased at the Reformation, but revived in the eighteenth century, which is paradoxical, because religion was then at a low ebb. This dignified building was the work of the Bastards, who were to restore Blandford after its fire of 1731.

In the main, Dissent appealed to merchants and traders, so the sects were strongest in the towns. They formed important minorities, while at Bridport they even took control of the corporation throughout the 18th century. The Test Act should have prevented this, but failed to do so because Bridport's Dissenters were willing to take communion in the parish church, something which would have been quite against the consciences of most members of their faith.

Catholics faced even more suspicion than Dissenters. As late as 1832 an election poster in Blandford read, 'Vote against Ponsonby, the Irishman who keeps a Popish Priest in his House.' George III was friendly with one of Dorset's leading Catholics, Thomas Weld of Lulworth Castle, whom he visited from time to time. Weld wanted to build a chapel and the king agreed, as long as it looked like a mausoleum from the outside. But though he would stretch a point for a friend, George III was against Catholic emancipation in principle. It was not until 1829 that Parliament passed an act giving Catholics full civil rights. Thomas Weld's son, another Thomas, was the first Englishman to be made a cardinal since the Reformation.

Boyle's School, Yetminster.

During the 18th century, more and more schools were founded for children of the poor. In 1791 the great chemist, Robert Boyle, endowed one at Yetminster to teach 20 poor boys. The school was working until 1949 and the building still stands. Boyle's school was for boys only, but some people were beginning to recognise that girls, too, should have an education. As early as 1640, Richard Foster had founded a school for 'Ten poore Boyes and Ten poore Maides' at Sherborne. Then, in 1743, Lord Digby founded a school for 13 poor girls. Wearing their blue uniforms, they sat in the Abbey opposite the children from Foster's School. Girls were expected to make good wives and mothers, so they usually had a different education from boys. At Bradford Abbas, for example, the boys learnt the 3Rs, but the girls learnt reading, spinning and knitting. They could, though, learn writing at Sunday school.

Even with the growing number of schools, only a minority of working class children attended, while those who did might not always have benefited as much as they should have done. Incomes from endowments were usually meagre, so teachers were allowed to take private pupils. By

146

1834 there were 26 poor boys at Boyle's School, but the master had also admitted 34 fee payers. There can be little doubt which group had the better attention.

In an attempt to reach all poor children, Sunday schools were opened. William Morton Pitt endowed one at Poole, investing £173 6s 8d in 3% consols. Any child could attend, regardless of denomination, and the teachers were not allowed to charge fees. The curriculum was modest, being only religion, spelling and reading, but this was realistic for a school that functioned just one day in the week. In 1837, 114 boys and 95 girls were attending this school.

Dorset's poor still depended, to quite an extent, on charities, and these grew in number. Blandford, which already had the so-called Church Almshouses, gained another set when George Ryves founded his 'gerontocomium' in 1682. It escaped the fire of 1731, is still standing and is still in use. The building is impressive, for it was meant to glorify the founder as well as shelter the poor. Inside, the dwellings are less attractive than from outside, though they are much better since the original ten were converted to five. The inmates were given their clothing and pensions of 2s 6d a week. Each poor person had to wear a silver badge, bearing a greyhound, which was Ryves's crest. The Reeves firm, which made paints and crayons, was founded by the same family and used the same greyhound as its crest.

Whether a town or village had ample charities and whether any particular individual could benefit from them was still a matter of luck. The only universal safety net remained the Poor Law. These extracts from the Blandford records tell their own story:

		£ s d
1728	Gave a poor woman heavy with child a shilling to go away	1 0
[This was to prevent the child becoming a charge on the parish.]		
1739	Paid for ye cure of John Pottles wife of ye itch	1 6
1742	Paid a months keeping Mary Shittler at the madhouse	1 0 0
1760	Paid Dr Dansey for cutting of Saml Tuckers leg	6 6 0
1775	Paid for carrying Sall Bad's child yt was left at my door back again	6

The administration of the poor law changed in the towns and some of the larger villages with the opening of workhouses. It had always been intended that able-bodied paupers should earn their keep, but setting them to repair roads or giving them materials to make up in their own homes had never been very successful. It was decided to put them to work under close supervision. The inmates of Blandford workhouse were ordered to make buttons and in 1770 there were eleven women and three men producing, between them, ten gross a day. In 1764 John Jenkins, a model pauper, made ten dozen on his own, but another time, Hannah Ellot lost just as many. Her kind was the more typical, so in general, workhouses as places of work were failures. Instead, they became refuges for orphans, the sick and the elderly.

A common way of disposing of orphans was to apprentice them. The parish would pay an employer a premium of something like £5 and the employer would agree to keep the child until it was 21 and teach it a trade. Thus, for a single payment, the parish was rid of a liability, while the employer had what was, in effect, a slave for several years. Few 'parish apprentices' learnt anything worthwhile and some were sent many miles from their friends and families, even as far as Newfoundland.

Crime flourished during the 18th century, most of it stealing and violence in their various forms. Punishments were still the pillory, the stocks, the whipping post, the branding iron and the gallows. There was even burning alive for a few offences, including petty treason, which was murder by someone in a position of trust, such as a wife or a servant. In 1705 a girl of 19 called Mary Channing fell victim to this law. Though she protested her innocence, she was convicted of poisoning her elderly husband, whom she had been forced to marry. Mary was allowed to wean a baby she had had by another man, and then taken to Maumbury Rings in Dorchester for her punishment. Out of pity, the executioner strangled her before lighting the fire. Ten thousand people watched.

A punishment that became quite usual was transportation. As we have seen, many of the Monmouth rebels were sent to the West Indies. In 1717, an Act of Parliament allowed convicted felons to choose transportation instead of branding, whipping or even hanging. The result was a trade in felons between Britain and the plantation colonies, sturdy criminals fetching up to £80 a time. The traffic came to an end after the American War of Independence broke out in 1775, but a new destination was soon found. In 1787 Commodore Perry set sail with two frigates and a fleet of transports bearing 800 convicts, bound for Botany Bay in New South Wales. A Poole man, Michael Dennison, was one of this band of reluctant pioneers.

18

RIOTERS AND MARTYRS

While the landed gentry of Dorset were spending fortunes on their houses and their estates, the poorest of the country folk were struggling to survive. Robert Grant, vicar of Bradford Abbas, wrote:

> They were ill paid, ill housed, ill fed and ill clad. And when sickness was added to poverty the burden which they had to bear was necessarily much heavier. My Parish formed no exception to the hard state and circumstances of the labouring classes in the County. The hard-earned wages of the ordinary farm labourer averaged 7s 0d per week, with some trifling perquisites.

There is evidence that enclosure sometimes hurt the poor. The people of Ringwood objected when their heath was planted with pine trees, as this robbed them of furze and turf for fuel. A farmer called Barrett had had the right to graze 15 oxen on the Great Common at Leigh, and when this was enclosed in 1804 he was awarded 15 acres. But only the very best of pasture would support oxen at the rate of one per acre so it is likely that he had to part with some of his beasts. We have seen that many of the small men at Beaminster were given allotments of half an acre each when their common was enclosed, and that some of them could not resist selling. When they had spent the money, they had neither common rights nor land.

Further, Robert Grant was right to be concerned about wages, for the population was increasing the whole time, resulting in such a surplus of labour that it drove down its price. On the other hand, the 'perquisites' which Grant mentions may have been more important than he would admit. When William Stevenson was preparing his report for the Board of Agriculture, he found that many farmers loaned their labourers potato patches, which they ploughed and manured for them. A plot might be anything from one sixth to one third of an acre and the yield could be anything up to 100 bushels. This allowed the family to keep a pig. When living, the animal provided manure for the cottage garden, which grew all manner of vegetables. When dead, it kept the family in meat for much of the year. In the chalk areas at least, it was common for farmers to sell their labourers bread corn cheaply and at a fixed price. This spared them one of the greatest worries that afflicted the poor in those days, which was a bad harvest leading to a steep rise in the price of bread, their staple food. Another perquisite, of more doubtful value, was drink. In the 1760s the manor house farm at Sandford Orcas was producing 4,000 gallons of cider a year, possibly 2½ gallons per labourer per week throughout the year.

The farmers' motives were mixed. One cynic told Stevenson that loaning his men potato patches meant they stayed with him through the summer, because otherwise they forfeited their crops. But another farmer sold his workers cheap corn to keep them out of the clutches of the hucksters. 'If they get in debt,' he said, 'it injures their moral character.'

In 1836 James Taylor, a farmer from Little Bredy, told a Parliamentary Select Committee that each of his labourers had a rent free cottage, a potato patch ploughed and manured, an allowance of wheat and a garden. All this, he thought, was worth 4s a week, raising a cash wage of 7s to a real wage of 11s.

Robert Grant said of his parishioners, 'The endurance and patience with which their lot was borne were as extraordinary as they were praiseworthy', and it is possible that the majority of farm workers would have gone on in a spirit of stoic resignation but for one thing, which was the introduction of threshing machines. Men were no longer needed to thresh with the flail through the winter, so some farmers dismissed all but their key workers until the spring. The result was the Swing Riots of 1830. They were given this name because many unpopular folk received letters signed by a mythical 'Captain Swing'.

The troubles began in Kent, where labourers hoisted a tricolor. By day, they gathered in mobs to smash threshing machines and duck poor law overseers in village ponds. By night, small groups set fire to ricks. The disorders were not planned but spread like a forest fire, one village rising when it heard that its neighbours had done so.

The first of the troubles in Dorset took place at Bere Regis on 22nd November 1830. A crowd gathered and James Frampton of Moreton harangued it, refusing to give in to demands or to be intimidated by threats. On 28th November, there was another gathering, this time of people from Winfrith, Wool and Lulworth, and again it was Frampton who confronted it. He was backed by some 150 farmers, who had enlisted as special constables. The crowd was peaceful enough, but refused to disperse even after the Riot Act had been read, so Frampton's men charged. Three protesters were arrested and sent to Dorchester for trial. Frampton himself grabbed a man, but he escaped by wriggling out of his smock. After that, Frampton received several threats, so he boarded the lower windows of his house and the Mayor of Dorchester sent some militia to defend it. There was no attack, and not even any fires on Frampton's estate.

The agent of the Bankes estate received the following letter:

> Mr Castleman, Sir, Sunday night your house shall come down to the ground for you are an inhuman monster and we will dash out your brains – Banks and your sett aught to be sent to hell. The Hanley Torches have not forgot you.

Again, these were empty threats.

Most of the troubles were in the north of the county. Gangs went from farm to farm demanding money and drink and smashing threshing machines. Some of the simpler fellows imagined they would be paid a bounty for every machine they destroyed. At night, ricks were burnt. But the rioters did not hurt anyone, all the damage being to property. James Read, who had three stolen sovereigns in his pocket, came to the aid of Lord Salisbury who was being attacked by a man with an iron bar. This action saved Read from transportation.

To deal with the rising, the county was split into divisions, Weymouth, Dorchester and Blandford. Each raised a force of special constables, Blandford having 200 mounted men and 2,000 foot. Others adopted Fabian tactics. Portman of Blandford agreed to increase wages, so making himself unpopular with the more determined landowners. Many farmers thought it prudent to dismantle their threshing machines before the rioters smashed them. Force and conciliation worked well at Cranborne, as the *Salisbury and Winchester Journal* reported:

> A large number of the inhabitants of Cranborne and the neighbour-hood were speedily sworn special constables. They, with a party of about 40 horse, headed by the Marquess of Salisbury, Mr Sturt and others, marched forward to meet the mob, whom they found engaged in burning a machine at Gussage. After much persuasion and remonstrance, they were at length prevailed on to retire to their abodes. The following day, a scale of higher wages was proposed to them, which had the effect of restoring tranquillity.

In January 1831 a Special Commission arrived in Dorchester to try the 55 men who had been arrested throughout the county. Six of them were sentenced to transportation. James Frampton's sister, Mary, noted in her diary, 'Care was taken to keep them separate from convicts of a different description and to send them where their agricultural knowledge and labour might be useful – thus rendering our disturbances a blessing to the Antipodes.'

The convictions for all those parts of England affected by the Swing Riots were nine hanged and 450 transported, which suggests that the troubles were not too serious in Dorset. None the less, they left the landowners nervous and the memory of them was still green when, in February 1834, a certain James Legg told the redoubtable Frampton that some men of Tolpuddle had formed a trade union.

The previous year, the labourers of the village had met the farmers and had won a promise of an increase in wages. Instead, the farmers had pleaded hardship and reduced the wages. This persuaded numbers of the men that they should join a union, and in December 1833 some 40 of them agreed to form a Friendly Society of Agricultural Labourers. Frampton and his kind had reason to be alarmed. They still had vivid memories of the Swing Riots, and they were suspicious of the men's leaders, several of whom had embraced Methodism, which was often a way of defying both parson and squire. More important, trade unions in those days seemed akin to revolutionary cells. They admitted their members in macabre ceremonies, binding them to secrecy with bloodcurdling oaths. Regalia discovered at Exeter included 'two wooden axes, two large cutlasses, two masks, two white robes, a large figure of Death with a dart and hour glass, a Bible and a Testament', hardly the adjuncts of peaceful bargaining. Further, the Tolpuddle men were ambitious. Their organisation was to be the Grand Lodge of a union that would have branches throughout Dorset. To cap it all, the Friendly Society of Agricultural Labourers was to be affiliated to the Grand National Consolidated Trades Union. This was the creation of Robert Owen who, though a mill owner, was one of the most radical socialists that England has produced. His aim was to enlist every worker in his union, which would paralyse the country with a general strike and then take over not only all factories and firms, but also the government, even superseding Parliament.

The landowners and farmers decided they must crush the union. There was, though, a problem, because trade unions had been legal ever since Parliament had repealed the Combination Acts in 1824. But the Home Secretary, Lord Melbourne, gave good advice. Some of the Tolpuddle men had taken secret oaths, which had been forbidden by an act of 1797 intended to help put down a naval mutiny. The dust was blown off the act and it was used to prosecute six men: George Loveless,

152

Thomas Standfield's cottage, Tolpuddle. Just beyond the cottage is the ruined Methodist chapel.

his brother James Loveless, their brother-in-law Thomas Standfield and his son John, James Brine, who was later to marry a Standfield, and James Hammett.

In March 1834 the six stood trial before Baron Williams at Dorchester. They were, of course, quite unaware of the act of 1797, but ignorance of the law is never a defence. Two labourers, John Lark and the informer Legg, described the oath taking, while a painter's wife said that her husband had drawn a picture of Death and another of a skeleton. In his statement, George Loveless said, 'My Lord, if we have violated any law, it was not done intentionally; we have injured no man's reputation, character, person or property; we were united to preserve ourselves, our wives and our children from utter degradation and starvation.' The court was not sympathetic. Summing up, Williams said that if trade unions continued they would 'ruin masters, cause a stagnation in trade and destroy property.' The jury, nearly all of them small farmers, returned a verdict of guilty in 20 minutes, and Williams gave the maximum sentence of seven years' transportation.

There was now an outcry throughout Britain, in which even the Tory press joined, glad of any excuse to attack the Whig government. Most support came from the Grand National Consolidated Trades Union which organised a meeting between 30,000 and 40,000 strong

Idealised view of the meeting of the Grand National Consolidated Trades Union in Copenhagen Fields, April 1834. This picture is on a plate presented to Thomas Wakely. (Mansell Collection)

in Copenhagen Fields and presented a monster petition to Parliament. But the days of the Union were numbered, for it collapsed within a year of its formation. However, the 'Dorchester Labourers' Committee' kept agitating and there was support from Thomas Wakley, MP for Finsbury. In June 1835, Wakley urged Parliament to present an address to the king, asking for a pardon, but this was opposed by the Home Secretary, Lord John Russell, and the motion was lost by 308 votes to 82. Wakley raised the question again in March 1836, and received a reply that must have baffled him completely. Lord John announced that the Tolpuddle men had already received a free pardon and would be coming home, first class, at the government's expense. The reason for this change of heart has never been discovered.

The promise of first class travel was not kept. Moreover, it took some time to return the men to England, for they were on farms at various places deep in Australia and communications were poor. The last to arrive home was James Hammett, in September 1837. No one, not even his fellow convicts, had taken the trouble to make sure he knew about his pardon, and he only found out when he read an old newspaper.

The 'Tolpuddle Martyrs' became the patron saints of the trade union movement. The TUC opened a museum in their village and preserves the Old Crown Court in Dorchester as a shrine to their memory.

19

THE RAILWAY AGE

Britain's first railways were built in the 16th century. They were privately owned mineral lines which linked mines and quarries to the nearest water transport. For traction, they used horses and gravity. Dorset's first mineral line was built in 1806. It belonged to Benjamin Fayle, a London potter, who used it to carry clay from Middlebere to the southern shore of Poole Harbour. Then, in 1826, the Merchants' Railway opened on the Isle of Portland. Horses drew trucks from the quarries to the top of Freeman's Incline, which was a precipitous drop of 400 feet, ending at Castledown Pier. The railway carried stone for six days of the week, and brought visitors to the prison on Sundays.

Most of Britain's main line railways were built during the 'railway mania' of the late 1840s, in which Dorset played a modest part. A Wimborne solicitor called Castleman thought he saw a splendid opportunity. Both the Great Western Railway and the London and South Western Railway wanted to make a direct link between London and Exeter. Castleman's plan was to form a company and obtain an Act of Parliament sanctioning a railway from Southampton to Dorchester. This would give him control of the territory through which the two giants wanted to pass, so that he could then play one against the other.

The Southampton to Dorchester opened in 1847, though it had little potential as a section of a great national railway, since it meandered across country to avoid estuaries and to link centres of population. People called it 'Castleman's Corkscrew'. It made a wide sweep north of Bournemouth, which was then unimportant, to run through Ringwood and Wimborne. A branch line joined it to Hamworthy.

The negotiations with the big companies were less successful than Castleman had hoped. They came to an agreement between themselves, so the only one left in the market was the LSWR. It took over the Southampton to Dorchester in 1848, but then decided on a more northerly route for its line to Exeter. 'Castleman's Corkscrew' made no progress west of Dorchester. The sequel was happier for Castleman

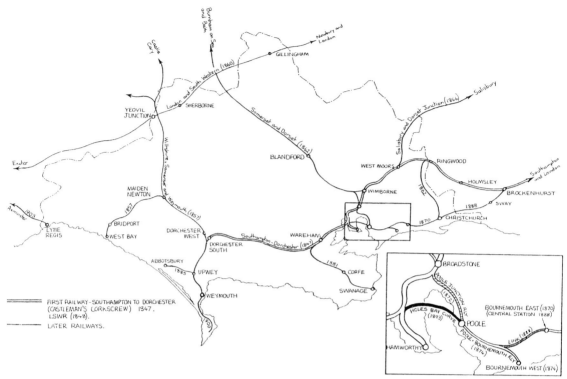

The map shows how Dorset's railways developed. (For railways in the 1990s, see page 7)

himself, who joined the board of the LSWR and was its chairman from 1873 to 1874.

The Wilts, Somerset and Weymouth Railway obtained its act in 1845, but was only completed with the help of the GWR in 1857. Eventually, it became part of the GWR network. It was built to Brunel's wide gauge of seven feet, but at Dorchester it encountered the LSWR, which had the 'standard' gauge of 4 foot 8½ inches. Accordingly, the Wilts, Somerset and Weymouth's Act required that the line between Dorchester and Weymouth should be dual gauge. That meant laying a third rail between the other two, in order to accommodate the LSWR trains. The same year that the railway was completed, the Weymouth and Channel Islands Steam Packet Company began its ferry services.

The Somerset and Dorset Railway was built to join the Bristol and English Channels. There were also to be steamers plying between Highbridge and Cardiff and between Poole and Cherbourg. There was, though, little demand for a service linking South Wales with northern France via rural Dorset, and the scheme was a failure. Then the Midland Railway reached Bath, and the S & D shot out a tentacle in that direction. The new branch from Evercreech opened in 1874.

London and South-Western Railway Locomotive No. 8 *Vesta*, by Sharp Roberts 1838. (Dorset County Museum)

Unfortunately it crossed the Mendip Hills, so there were some steep gradients. A railway historian has commented, 'It was always one of the joys and sorrows of the S & D that even the wind blowing over the Mendips could profoundly affect speed.'

Today, the railway from Waterloo to Weymouth passes through Christchurch, Bournemouth, Poole and Dorchester, so linking Dorset's principal towns with each other and with London. Nothing could seem more logical, yet the story of the eastern section is complicated.

In the 1840s Bournemouth was still too insignificant to attract a railway, which meant it was difficult to reach. A traveller wrote:

> After exploring what seemed to me the whole of the South Coast, I finally reached Hamworthy. A porter informed me that Bournemouth was five miles further. He had never been there, but there was a good road and I had better go by Oxford. The mystery was solved by the driving up of a little old omnibus, owned by 'G. Axford', who conveyed passengers once a day to Bournemouth.

When, finally, Bournemouth was large enough to merit a railway, most of its élite inhabitants resisted the idea, and though the railway did reach the town, it only did so by a slow process of infiltration. The opening of the two stations was not as decisive as might appear, since they were both well away from the town centre, while the line between Ringwood and Christchurch was so badly made that trains were limited to 25 mph.

The link with Brockenhurst through Sway and the joining of the stations were important developments, and the opening of the Holes Bay Curve in 1893 meant that direct through traffic was at last possible.

The railway embankments, cuttings and tunnels were made by gangs of navvies, whose work was both hard and dangerous. In the Dorset newspapers there were reports of men crushed by trucks and buried in tunnels. As the railways progressed, so the navvies moved with them, towns and villages dreading their arrival as much as if they had been a foreign army. To any clergyman worth his salt, though, they were a splendid opportunity to try his missionary skills without the trouble of voyaging to Africa or the Far East. The Rev Robert Grant of Bradford Abbas wrote a lively account of his dealings with the navvies building the Salisbury to Yeovil line. At first he made mistakes, such as asking the names and places of origin of men who were, quite likely, wanted by the police, but on the whole he was tactful. He started by exchanging greetings, and then offered water from his well, as well as his services as a letter writer. From there, he advanced to prayer meetings and the distribution of testaments. Generally, the navvies committed few crimes, but they did sire numbers of bastards.

The arrival of a railway could transform a place. Maiden Newton found itself at the junction between the Wilts, Somerset and Weymouth Railway and the branch line to Bridport. Its sheep and cattle market revived, while numerous tradesmen prospered, along with a foundry and a tannery. The railway itself provided work, for there were various station officials and several porters.

Gillingham became an industrial town in miniature. It already had a silk mill, founded in 1769 and it acquired a gas works in 1837. Ten years later, the Oake-Woods bacon factory opened, using a method of curing bacon under pressure that was later adopted by the Danes. Then, in 1859, the railway arrived and over the years a range of industries appeared. A brick and tile works opened, using the local Kimmeridge clay, and there were two butter and cheese factories, a brewery, a saw mill, two printing works, a workshop making bicycles, an engineering company making stationary petrol engines and a soap works. As a complement to the brewery, there was a mineral water factory producing lemonade, soda water, ginger beer and ginger wine.

The railways had their most drastic effect on the seaside towns, which became popular resorts. This happened to Weymouth quite early and Bournemouth succumbed, eventually. Even Swanage, with its uncouth quarrymen, became a resort after the arrival of the railway in 1881. Most of the visitors were on day excursions, for there were no paid holidays. Excursion trains were not the swiftest, and, in a long, hard day, the people must have spent twice as much time in them as they did on the beach. However, in 1910 a train known as the 'Pines Express' began a regular service from Manchester to Bournemouth. Its passengers were very different from the crowds who flocked to the coast for the day.

The railways had varied effects on the roads. Few people would take a coach if there was a train, but it was some time before the railways were finished and, in the meantime, coaches filled the gaps. In the early 1850s, for example, the *Prince Albert* coach ran between the terminus of Castleman's Corkscrew at Dorchester and Yeovil on the London to Exeter line.

Later, as the railways multiplied, long distance coach travel declined and the turnpike trusts were wound up, one by one. The last in Dorset, Blandford's, ended in 1883. But even when the railways were completed, they had not reached some of the towns and most of the villages, so the inhabitants of these places still had to travel between them by horse or on foot as they always had done. The railways also generated a good deal of business, so it is likely that they created more road traffic than they killed.

In 1888 a Local Government Act introduced county councils, which at once took over the roads. At about this time cycling became popular, especially after the 'safety bicycle' replaced the penny farthing in the 1880s, and Dunlop invented the pneumatic tyre. The first motor cars appeared towards the end of the century.

'Castleman's Corkscrew' destroyed Poole's coastal trade almost at once. Sixty-four ships were engaged in it in 1847, but within five years there were none. Help, though, was at hand. Bournemouth's population grew from 691 in 1851 to 16,859 in 1881 and Poole imported much that was needed by its neighbour, including grain, timber and roofing slate. In 1893, the quay was extended eastwards and outwards, to reach deeper water. The port, though, was far from being one of Britain's leaders. Even at the turn of the century, steamers passed it by and it was sailing ships that lined the quay.

British industry grew remarkably during the railway age, but mainly on the coal fields. Dorset had no coal so progress here was modest.

Portland stone was quarried in growing quantities and with the help of some new workers. A prison was built on the Isle in 1848 so that convicts could build a breakwater, making a harbour for the Royal Navy. A great deal of stone was used in the Nothe and the Verne, the two great fortresses that defended the harbour. People made excursions to Portland so that they could see the convicts returning to prison in chains at the end of the day.

The beds of Portland stone continue into the Isle of Purbeck. The so-called 'Purbeck Portland' is less attractive than the genuine Portland, but is harder. Farmers used it for drinking troughs, rollers and staddle stones, but it had more important uses in such works as bridges and docks. Up to 50,000 tons a year were quarried.

Due to faulting and folding the Purbeck Portland stone comes to the surface in several places and here open cast working was possible. Later there were drift mines, in which the galleries sloped downwards from the surface as they followed the strata. This stone went to Swanage by cart, where it was stacked in 'bankers'. High-wheeled carts took it into the sea, and it was then loaded into barges that took it to the ships. In its journey from quarry to ship it was handled five times, though loading became more efficient after 1860, when a pier was built with a tramway from the bankers.

Much Purbeck stone was won from the cliff faces. The first stage was 'ridding', which meant blasting away an enormous slice of cliff to make a wide ledge. This was used as a quay, where stone could be stacked, and from where it could be lowered into barges that took it to Swanage. The quarrymen drove their galleries straight into the cliffs, creating artificial caves. In the quarries, children worked and died. An old quarryman explained, 'They wuss cheap, plenny of 'em, an' more wurr they come vrom.'

The two most important men in the Purbeck stone industry were John Mowlem and his nephew, George Burt. They sent much of their stone to London and, needing return cargoes, would sometimes buy an old building, take it apart and then put it together again in Swanage. The town became known as 'Little London by the Sea'. Some Portland stone that went to London in the mid 17th century became the façade of the Mercers' Hall; it now adorns the front of Swanage Town Hall.

Dorset's other traditional extractive industry, clay, not only grew but spawned some manufacturing. As the population increased more houses were needed, so there was a demand for bricks, tiles and drain pipes. Clay pits were opened in many parts of the county. The railways had needed millions of bricks themselves, and now they returned the favour with a steady supply of coal for the kilns. At various times there were 75 clay pits within the Poole boundaries, though few of them were worked for very long. In Hamworthy, the South Western Pottery made fancy chimney pots and door and window surrounds in terracotta. There are examples at the western entrance to Poole Park.

The output of ball clay also expanded, 15,000 tons being exported from Poole in 1802 and 63,000 in 1859. More mineral lines were built on Purbeck and they had diminutive steam locomotives to pull the trains. There was also a steam tug, which towed the barges to Poole.

Horse whin for pulling stone out of mine, Durleston.

Ball clay is a bonding agent in ceramics, but only a little is needed in each article which meant that for a long time it was most economical to make pottery on the Staffordshire coalfield. However, better communications meant it was cheaper to bring coal and china clay to Poole, and in 1873 Jesse Carter opened a pottery on the quay, to manufacture tiles. Thousands of Carter tiles line the London Underground. Jesse's son Owen later increased the firm's range of goods.

A new extractive industry was the exploitation of iron ore on Hengistbury Head, where it occurs in boulders known as 'doggers'. In the 1840s they attracted the attention of a Christchurch coal merchant called Holloway who traded with South Wales and needed a return cargo. The doggers suited him admirably, for they were over 30% iron and commanded a good price.

Holloway quarried the north slope of Warren Hill, making a gash that all but cut the Head in two. He also took doggers from the shore on the south side. They had been protecting the cliffs which now crumbled into the sea, so that a third of the Head was lost and much of Bournemouth's beach was swept round into Christchurch Bay. Christchurch would have been exposed to the sea had Holloway destroyed the Head, but he was popular in the town because he had brought work to it. He was elected to the council and became mayor in 1867. Only Druitt, the Town Clerk

161

fought against him. With help from Bournemouth, Druitt stopped the removal of ironstone in 1870, by which time Holloway had made himself a fortune.

Bridport's rope and net industries and East Dorset's button making all thrived in the first half of the 19th century, but their fortunes were very different in the second half.

Button making was in the hands of merchants like the Cases who did nothing to improve the technology of their industry. They had fair warning, since in 1810 a Dane called Sanders had opened a factory in Birmingham which mass produced wire buttons. Sanders covered his buttons with paste board, so they did not survive many washes and the Dorset merchants saw no cause for alarm. Then, in 1850, Sanders's son-in-law, Ashton, patented a machine that would cover the wire rings with cloth. Henry Case described what happened to his business:

> The smash came at last, 1851–2–3, worse and worse. We employed in wire makers, paperers and button workers from 800 to 1,000; but they were soon in a state of poverty, some starving, and hundreds were sent off to Perth, Moreton Bay and Quebec by the noblemen of the county. In 1850 there was on hand a stock of £14,500 worth of goods and buttons; but my uncle still continued his journeys to the chief towns. In March 1859, I sold in the City £856 worth of wire and cloth worked buttons in five days, and that was the last extensive sale of the hand-made button.

Case and his colleagues had waited until disaster was upon them, whereupon they simply redoubled their efforts at marketing. Inevitably, this was to no avail.

The Bridport industries, in contrast to buttony, were in the hands of men who showed plenty of enterprise. Dorset hemp and flax are not of the highest quality, so the manufacturers began importing these materials from the Baltic. After 1850 there were machines for hackling, combing and rope spinning, with power looms to weave sails. For nets they had the 'jumping loom', so named because at the end of each cycle the operator had to jump with his full weight on a pedal. Meanwhile, the women outworkers concentrated on finer goods, like the pockets for billiard tables. Some of this 'braiding' as they called it, was real artwork. Firms amalgamated for extra strength and to raise capital for machines, and the rope and net industries not only survived, but flourished.

Lord Ernle, the agricultural historian, described the third quarter of the 19th century as the 'golden age of British farming'. In part,

A small rural dairy in Dorset around the turn of the century. (Dorset County Museum)

this success was due to the railways, for livestock and produce could be transported quickly and cheaply. Dorset butter no longer went to London in lumbering waggons, while cattle and sheep travelled by train, instead of meandering for days along green roads, losing weight with every step. Fresh milk could now be sent long distances, if the farm was near a railway. The platform at Gillingham station had to be lengthened to take all the churns.

Demand also increased, for not only had the towns grown, but many of their people enjoyed higher wages. No longer having to subsist on bread, potatoes and the occasional herring, they sometimes bought dairy produce and meat. This demand was met by improved methods, Dorset's farmers being among the most progressive in the country.

Dorset's best known farmer of the period was the Rev Anthony Huxtable, who was rector of Sutton Waldron for 37 years. His Hill Farm attracted visitors from all over the country including the writer on agriculture, James Caird. Caird has left an enthusiastic account of what he found.

Hill Farm was 280 acres of chalk down, where Huxtable grew wheat and barley, alternated with green crops such as turnips, swedes, mangolds, rye grass, vetches and clover. To work the fields Huxtable had 'cultivators, scarifiers, clodcrushers, seed-drills, dibbling machines, and a liquid-manure-and-seed-drill.' It was the buildings, though, that interested Caird the most, 'the meat and manure factory of the farm' he called them. Only the breeding ewes went out to graze, the cattle, sheep and pigs being 'constantly housed night and day'. The animals stood on slatted floors, through which their urine ran, to be carefully collected. Solid manure was picked up with the straw. Not a drop of the one nor a scrap of the other was wasted.

The farm's steam engine threshed and winnowed corn, cut chaff, ground cattle food and crushed bones. The waste heat from the fire dried corn, while the steam exhaust softened the chaff.

Another use for steam engines was ploughing. A traction engine was put on one side of the field and a pulley was anchored at the other. The engine then drew the plough from side to side, on the end of a cable, stirring the soil far more deeply than horses could have done. The method was especially suitable on the chalk, where the fields were large. As the equipment was too expensive for the average farmer, the work was done by contractors, like the Dorchester Steam Plough Works.

An important capital improvement was land drainage, which was easier after about 1850 when clay pipes were being mass produced. But drainage was still expensive, and had to be done with care if it was to be effective.

Such, then, was 'high farming'. Unfortunately, the railways which had helped create it were also partly responsible for its ruin. They opened up the temperate grasslands of the world and farmers on these virgin soils produced food at much lower prices than was possible in Britain. After 1875 there was a flood of wheat from the North American prairies, which was later joined by frozen meat from New Zealand. British farming went into a decline that was to last, with an intermission during the First World War, until 1939.

20

PROBLEMS AND PROGRESS

During the Victorian period, no institutions were more important than the churches, for this was an age of faith. There was a climate of opinion which favoured religion, and this was fostered by the clergy who, in contrast with many of their eighteenth century predecessors, were dedicated men. Alfred Austin, one of the Commissioners who prepared the *Report on Women and Children in Agriculture*, 1843, wrote:

> I nearly everywhere found the clergy attempting to improve the condition of the labouring population. They are nearly always the main supporters, and frequently the managers of the clothing clubs, coal clubs etc; they are commonly the promoters of education, and of improvements in the schools; whilst their wives not infrequently devote much of their time to visiting the cottages, and advising and helping the women in their difficulties.

The Victorians' religious zeal led them to build new churches, as well as to restore and extend many they had inherited. Gussage All Saints acquired a new chancel in the 1860s. At Sandford Orcas in 1871, the chancel arch was taken down to be rebuilt on proper foundations, and a north aisle was added. The incumbent at Blandford found the apse cramped his style, so he wanted a chancel. To make room for it, the architect, Charles Hunt, sliced the apse from the main building, moved it 30 feet to the east with the aid of jacks and rollers, and then deposited it, still intact, on new foundations.

Some of the new churches replaced old ones that had crumbled beyond repair, like West Lulworth. Others were built in places where the population was growing, such as Poole's new suburbs and, as we shall see, Bournemouth.

Much Victorian church restoration was ham-fisted and insensitive, but without it, there would not have been as many medieval churches left to admire. The tower of St Peter's, Stourton Caundle, had no foundations other than some flat slabs a foot below the surface and resting on clay. As a result, the tower tilted towards the east, damaging the walls and roof of the nave. Repairs began at the turn of the century, the patron, Sir Henry Hoare, agreeing to meet much of the expense. Hoare insisted, though, that the building should be preserved. 'This offer,' he said, 'will not hold good for the purpose of pulling down and rebuilding the Church.'

The Nonconformist religions thrived along with the Anglican, spreading rapidly in the countryside, where formerly they had not been strong. Cottages once used as meeting houses were no longer big enough and, poor though the communities were, most of them built chapels. Many humble folk disliked their village church because it was dominated by their 'betters', the squire, the parson and the richer farmers. In the chapels, on the other hand, everyone was welcome, everyone was equal and there was little formality. Nor were people alienated by the 'hell-fire' preachers who described the agonies of the damned in such graphic detail that they scared the wits out of their congregations, especially the children among them.

Methodism was the most popular of the Nonconformist sects. It was particularly strong in Portland where, if the *Penny Magazine* is to be believed, it had great influence on the quarrymen. An article of 1836 gives a glowing account of them, commenting, 'The strongest oath and common expletive is "on the word of a Portland man".'

Generally, church and chapel co-existed without too much friction, but there was open hostility between Protestants and Roman Catholics. The Irish problems rumbled on and the Romish leanings of the Tractarian Movement in the Church of England caused alarm. Xenophobia played a part too, for the Pope was a foreigner. In 1850 Pius IX established a hierarchy of bishops in England, which was seen as papal aggression. The reports of the Dorset Protestant Society show the strength of feeling. They mention addresses against Popery, like that on *Romish persecutions at Madeira* given by the Rev R. S. Smith. There were also references to 'endeavours made at Spetisbury to deliver the inhabitants from the snares of Popery, which resulted in the discomfiture of a Popish priest'; ironically, there were complaints about 'the gross intolerance by which the Protestants of Chideock are oppressed.'

The last remark was directed against the Welds, who had remained loyal to their faith since the Reformation. They bought Chideock from their fellow Catholics, the Arundels, in 1802. In 1870 Charles Weld built the church of Our Lady of Martyrs and St Ignatius, not only designing it himself, but even carving some of the capitals.

Religious zeal, together with political rivalry, led to the reform of institutions, including Parliament. Before 1832, the Dorset county franchise was the same as in all the other counties of England, only 'forty shilling freeholders' having the right to vote. These were men who owned property which, if let, would have earned at least £2 rent a year. Town franchises varied. At Bridport, Corfe, Dorchester, Shaftesbury and Wareham those paying 'scot and lot', or local taxes, had the vote. Only council members could vote at Christchurch, and they were not even elected themselves. At Poole and Lyme Regis the freemen were enfranchised, but they were only a tiny minority of the inhabitants. Weymouth-Melcombe Regis had much the same franchise as the county.

Electorates were small in all the towns and there was no secret ballot, so it was easy enough to win votes by bribery or intimidation. In the 'pocket boroughs', not even that was necessary and a century or more could go by without an election being contested. There was a cosy arrangement at Corfe whereby the Bankes family, which was Tory, nominated one member, and the Bond family of Creech Grange, which was Whig, nominated the other. Lord Shaftesbury and Lord Ilchester had a similar arrangement at Shaftesbury, though a third candidate did present himself in 1774. That year the official candidates, if they can be so called, had to pay the voters 20 guineas each in order to win their seats. The Rose family controlled Christchurch, while at Lyme Regis the Fanes ruled with a rod of iron.

There were advantages for the towns in all this. Two of Poole's MPs built a splendid guildhall, and it was only one of a series of gifts from grateful representatives. In 1739 Thomas Missing provided a workhouse at the cost of £500. In the 1780s William Morton Pitt presented the borough with 'a magnificent pair of maces to be borne before the mayor, and with two superb glass chandeliers for the guildhall.' As late as 1830, Benjamin Lester and W. F. S. Ponsonby gave the town its first library building. At Shaftesbury, a hopeful candidate laid out Park Walk, surely one of the most delightful election bribes ever given.

The parliamentary system was such that it gave the landed interest a complete monopoly of the House of Lords and an almost complete monopoly of the House of Commons. This led to growing discontent in the early 19th century especially among powerful new men, such as the industrialists of the north of England, where several large towns were not represented. In March 1831 Lord Grey's Whig government introduced a Reform Bill, but it was defeated in the Commons. After a general election, a second Reform Bill passed the Commons, but was thrown out by the Lords. This was in October, and it was followed by disturbances in many parts of England, Dorset included. One mob

167

rioted in Parkstone, of all places, while another smashed the windows of Sherborne Castle. The worst trouble, though, was at Blandford where a crowd smashed the windows of almost every anti-reformer in the town, ransacked the offices of two lawyers and demolished several houses.

Eventually, and only after a constitutional crisis, a Reform Act was passed in June 1832. The county franchise was extended to include the wealthier tenant and leasehold farmers. As they depended on the landowners for their farms and there was still no secret ballot, this measure increased the influence of the landed aristocracy. The town franchises were made uniform, with the middle classes, defined as occupants of buildings worth £10 a year, having the vote. This was hardly democratic; Poole, for example, with a population of 8,300, still had an electorate of only 412. Finally, there was a fairer, if still imperfect, distribution of seats. The places who gained were the industrial towns, with their Whig ruling classes. Dorset lost, though it still had 14 members while its population would have entitled it to no more than six.

The following table shows the changes that were made in the nineteenth century:

Parliamentary representation in Dorset

	Before 1832	1832	1867
County members	2	3	3
Bridport	2	2	1
Corfe Castle	2	–	–
Dorchester	2	2	1
Lyme Regis	2	1	–
Poole	2	2	1
Shaftesbury	2	1	1
Wareham	2	1	1
Weymouth-Melcombe Regis	4	2	1

After 1885, Poole was the only town returning a member. The rest of the county was divided into four one-member constituencies.

Many Dorset folk were unhappy with the 1832 Reform Act. There was a reluctance amongst some to accept that elections would no longer be opportunities for brawling, taking bribes and consuming unlimited free beer. Lyme Regis went on much as before, so earning the attentions of two Parliamentary commissions of enquiry and a comment in *The Times* that it was 'the most infamous sewer in British politics.' The old spirit lingered in Poole too, as is shown by this extract from the diary of Lady Charlotte Guest, wife of the lord of the manor, Sir John Guest. She describes the election of 1850:

> There was some hard fighting among the mob, and it was a sad scene to look down upon, very disgusting and degrading in my opinion. This was bad enough. I little contemplated what followed. As soon as Capt Parrot tried to speak, he was interrupted by every imaginable noise, and presently a rotten egg was thrown at him, which took very full effect. This was the first. It was followed by a regular volley mingled with apples, turnips and even stones. The uproar was tremendous. Seeing the stones, of which however only a few were mingled with the other missiles, I feared it must end badly and that someone would be injured. But fortunately something put it into the head of the mob to carry on their pelting with balls of flour, which were very innocent though their effect was very ludicrous, the flour sticking where the eggs had already taken effect and giving all the party on the hustings the appearance of being so many millers.

Such scenes came to an end after Gladstone secured the secret ballot in 1872, which he did in spite of warnings that it would 'sap the manly independence of the British voter.'

After Parliament had reformed itself, it reformed local government by the Municipal Corporations Act of 1835.

In the 18th century, many towns were ruled by 'closed corporations'. When a member of such a corporation died or went away, the survivors, and they alone, chose his successor. On the whole, closed corporations governed well, but they had become anachronisms, and, more to the point, they tended to be Tory. The Whigs were determined to be rid of them and the 1835 Act transferred their property and their powers to councils elected by the ratepayers.

In Poole the result of the act was to unleash strife and chaos. The town lost its admiralty jurisdiction giving it control over the harbour, so the fishermen immediately cleared the oyster beds. Worse followed.

At the first election, held in 1836, the Tories won, whereupon the Reformers accused them of irregularities and asked Parliament to declare the election void. The bill passed the Commons, but was flung out by the Lords. The Poole Tories celebrated, but the town's magistrates were Reformers and householders soon discovered they could withhold their rates with impunity, because the court would not enforce payment. There were also dark stories of a conspiracy. It was said that the Tories had rigged the election in order to dismiss their friend the Town Clerk, Robert Parr, so opening the way for him to sue for damages. The plot was probably not as deep as that, but the Council did, indeed, dismiss Parr, and he sued. He conducted his case so well that, during the tortuous legal proceedings, he won control of all the bankrupt Council's property, including the Guildhall, the regalia and the town gaol. Eventually, the Court of Chancery decided in Parr's favour, the judge remarking, 'I should be very glad to see this business settled. It is the most foolish dispute I have ever seen.' Foolish it might have been, but it had paralysed the government of the town for over a decade.

One of the achievements of the 19th century was to provide a school place for everyone. It had seemed a daunting problem, since there were few teachers and little money, but religion provided the spur while a new teaching method seemed, for a time, to supply the answer.

The arrival of Andrew Bell as rector of Swanage in 1801 was important for education in the country as a whole. Bell had been superintendent of the Madras Male Orphan Asylum, where, with hardly any resources, he had had to educate large numbers of children. To solve this problem he used the older and brighter children to teach the others. His young teachers were called 'monitors'. They came to school early and were taught what they had to teach. When the rest of the children arrived, each monitor took a small group and passed on what he had learnt. The master supervised, only intervening when necessary.

In 1802 Bell began employing monitors in the Swanage Sunday schools, and a master called Gover introduced Bell's system to his day school. Bell, not the most modest of men, wrote, 'It is like magic; order and regularity started up all at once. In half an hour more was learned and far better than had been done the whole day before.'

People were enthralled by Bell's idea. Here was a cheap and apparently efficient way of teaching, so that universal education at last seemed possible. There was, moreover, some urgency. A Quaker called Joseph Lancaster had developed the monitorial system independently of Bell, and in 1808 this led to the formation of the British and Foreign Schools Society. The Society was dominated by Nonconformists, so it seemed to the leaders of the Church of England that they were in danger of losing the souls of the nation's children. Accordingly, in 1811, Bell and other Anglicans formed the National Society for the Promotion of the Education of the Poor in the Principles of the Established Church. Three years later, the Society had 230 schools and over 40,000 pupils.

The schools affiliated to the two rival societies were known as 'British' and 'National', the chief difference between them being the religion they taught. The Nonconformists who ran the British Schools were content with non-denominational Christianity, which meant children from all their sects could attend. The Anglicans, on the other hand, insisted on teaching their own faith.

The dread of the Church of England clergy was that British Schools would appear in their parishes, so many of them provided National Schools. Usually, the lord of the manor gave most of the money, the incumbent made a large contribution and local farmers and gentry supplied the balance. Each of these worthy folk also promised to make an annual subscription towards the school's running expenses, while the parents were expected to pay a penny or twopence a week for each child. National Schools appeared in many Dorset villages, starting with Buckland Newton in 1816.

In 1835 Parliament began making annual grants for education. The money was paid directly to the schools and soon became their main source of income. However, leaving the provision of schools to voluntary agencies meant that supply was patchy, so in 1870 Parliament passed an Education Act 'to fill in the gaps left by the voluntary system'. The ratepayers of any town or village which did not have enough school places were to elect a School Board which would levy a rate to pay for the deficiency. Further, the Board Schools, as they were called, were forbidden to teach any 'religious catechism or religious formulary distinctive of any particular denomination.' Anglicans now faced a threat much more serious than the one from the British Schools, so they built frantically. The managers of any British School, on the other hand, were likely to be happy with the Act, and willing to surrender their school to their local Board, if there was one. The burden of maintaining the school then fell on the ratepayers, including the Anglicans among them.

Developments at Swanage were interesting because they were not entirely typical of Dorset, for there was no dominant landlord, while many of the inhabitants were quarrymen and Nonconformists. Bell left Swanage in 1809 and the town was to be without a National School for some years. Instead, the leading Nonconformists founded a British School which opened in 1832 with 50 boys and ten girls. This goaded the rector, Thomas Bartlett, into action. In 1836 he raised £200 for a building and gave glebe land for a site. The new school was, primarily, a Sunday School, but it taught infants during the week.

In 1854 Robert Duncan Travers, 'the building rector', arrived and he provided a school room for older children. Later, this acquired a porch 'for caps and bonnets', and gas lighting. However, an inspector of the local Board of Health said of the privies: 'Jammed into an unventilated corner, and close to the school building, their position is

Great Globe at Durlston Head, Swanage. The stone merchant, George Burt, turned Durlston Head into a recreational centre for the people of Swanage. But he was determined that their visits should be educational, so he provided all sorts of geographical information, carved in stone. This globe is the prime exhibit. It is made from sections, like an orange.

the worst that could be chosen, and their neglected state is evidenced by an inconceivably sickening stench.'

Swanage had enough school places in 1870 to avoid a School Board, so the Nonconformists were unable to dispose of their British School. Instead they seem to have let it die, for there are no references to it after 1871.

It had soon become clear that monitors did not make good teachers, so most schools employed pupil teachers. These were apprentices who began their training at twelve and qualified, if they finished the course, at 20. They were more use than monitors, though they sometimes gave trouble. At Swanage, complaints about them included hitting the children, climbing the school wall and staying away to hunt for a stray cow. By the end of the century there were enough qualified teachers for most schools to have one or two adult assistants.

As the population of Swanage grew, so the managers of the National School tried to keep pace with it. They added two classrooms to the main school room and enlarged the infants' school, but it was not enough. By the early 1890s there were 234 children on the registers, but places for only 196. The Nonconformists now demanded a School Board, and they had the support of George Burt, the quarry owner, who complained of the 'episcopalian' nature of the existing school. The rector, Thomas Gurney, fulminated, 'I shall not be to blame when the rate collector calls,' but he could not raise the money he needed. Swanage had its School Board and, moreover, the National School was surrendered to it in 1894. The Board supplied the extra places the town needed by opening a new school at Mount Scar in 1897.

There was a National School at Herston, a suburb of Swanage, and Anglicans in the neighbourhood rushed to its rescue when they saw what had happened in the main town. Thus, a school teaching the religion of the Church of England survived in a place where most of the inhabitants were Nonconformists.

Secondary education during the 19th century was given in the old endowed grammar schools and in private schools, both the preserves of the middle classes. The grammar schools stagnated for a long time. An act of 1840 allowed the courts to free them from their statutes, if they so wished, but most of them clung to the antiquated curricula which their founders had prescribed for them in the 16th and 17th centuries. That meant they spent most of their time on Latin, with just a few subsidiary subjects. By the middle of the century they were being a little more venturesome. Dorchester Grammar School had a headmaster who taught classics, a mathematics master and a master for drawing and French. Queen Elizabeth's School, Wimborne, had a headmaster and

Gillingham Grammar School,

DORSET.

founded 1526. Re-built 1873.

EXTENSIVE and MODERN PREMISES.

CRICKET AND FOOTBALL FIELDS.

COVERED FIVES COURTS AND LARGE GYMNASIUM.

NEW LABORATORIES
For the Teaching of Science
have lately been Built.

Boys prepared for the Universities, the Oxford and Cambridge Locals, College of Preceptors, etc.

For Prospectus, List of Successes, etc., apply to THE HEADMASTER.

DORCHESTER
Grammar School.

FOUNDED 1569.   REBUILT 1882.

CLASSICAL AND MODERN.

Chemical and Physical Laboratories recently built and equipped, and acknowledged to be the best in the County.

Workshop. Large Cricket and Football Field with New Pavilion.
EXCELLENT ACCOMMODATION FOR BOARDERS.

Large Dormitories with Separate Cubicles.
Isolated Sick Ward.

☞ SANITARY ARRANGEMENTS PERFECT. ☜

For particulars apply to

Head Master : S. A. ROOTHAM.

Advertisements for Grammar Schools, 1900.

an undermaster, both of whom taught classics, a mathematics master and a master for drawing and modern languages. The headmaster of Bridport Grammar School offered what he was pleased to call 'the usual branches of a complete English education', namely mathematics, Hebrew, German, Greek, Latin and French.

There were plenty of hard-headed businessmen who had no time for the grammar schools, but wanted their sons to learn something useful. Private schools filled this need, and faced with such competition the grammar schools had to modernise their curricula, as the advertisements of Dorchester and Gillingham Grammar Schools show.

Both Poole and Sherborne lost their grammar schools, but in very different ways. Poole's simply decayed until it was teaching only elementary subjects, and then closed in 1835. At Sherborne, an ambitious head, H. D. Harper, took advantage of the coming of the railway to open his doors to boarders from all over the country. According to the statutes, local boys were allowed to attend free and governors had to be local men, but, thanks to the Endowed Schools Act of 1869, Harper was able to avoid both these conditions. Sherborne School was highly successful, but it had ceased to be Sherborne's school. Foster's School, which had been founded for children of the poor, seized the opportunity to promote itself to Foster's Grammar School.

In 1902 Parliament passed an Education Act which abolished School Boards and made the County and County Borough Councils the Local

Education Authorities. They took over the Board Schools, which became 'Council Schools'. To the fury of the Nonconformists, any voluntary school which allowed the local authority to nominate a third of its managers would have its teachers' salaries paid out of the rates. The new authorities were also empowered to 'supply or aid the supply of education other than elementary', which led to the founding of state secondary schools. Poole and Weymouth, neither of which had an old endowed grammar school, both acquired secondary schools as a result of the Act.

From the end of the 18th century the cost of poor relief had soared in the country as a whole, including Dorset. Expenditure in Poole, for example, was £638 in 1770 and an average of £4,530 for the five years from 1815 to 1820. According to a Royal Commission on the Poor Laws this was due, largely, to people drawing poor relief when they were quite able to work. Dealing with the 'able-bodied pauper' became an obsession and, in 1834, Parliament passed the Poor Law Amendment Act. Parishes were ordered to form Poor Law Unions, so that they could pool their resources. One of the main duties of the new Unions was to build workhouses, which would make life so miserable for their inmates that those who could find work would do so.

The Poole Union consisted of the town itself, Hamworthy, Lytchett Minster, Lytchett Matravers, and Canford Magna, which included Parkstone and Longfleet. Poole already had its own workhouse, but this was not big enough for the Union, so a new one was begun almost at once at Longfleet. Other workhouses soon appeared, for example at Dorchester, Wareham, Weymouth and Bridport. All were solid buildings and all became hospitals when the Welfare State superseded the Poor Laws. At Blandford the Guardians kept the old workhouse for a time, so that the young, the old, the sick, the healthy and the insane all lived together. A new workhouse was not built until 1858.

A problem with the new Poor Law was that it did not differentiate between the idlers, who were a minority, and those in genuine need, such as orphans and the elderly. All suffered under the same harsh regime. At Dorchester, the women spent much of their time sitting on benches round the dining room and to emphasise their shame, they had to wear a uniform. They had no night clothes. When it was suggested that the paupers should have baths, some of the Guardians were indignant. One of them rolled up his sleeve, displayed his forearm and exclaimed, 'White as a hare's tooth, and hasn't been washed in 40 years!'

21

VICTORIAN TOWN AND COUNTRYSIDE

Dorset's towns reproduced all the evils of the industrial north, the only difference being one of scale. Dorchester will serve as an example. The population increased and there were some improvements, which created wide, handsome streets, but also destroyed the homes of numbers of poor folk. The town had a special problem in that it was hemmed in by land belonging to the Duchy of Cornwall, none of which was available for building. The only spare ground was a few acres in Fordington, which were soon covered in slums.

The poor of Fordington had a champion in their vicar, the Rev Henry Moule. He laid much of the blame for the misery of his people on the Duchy of Cornwall and wrote some forthright letters to the President of its Council, who was Victoria's consort, Prince Albert. Moreover, he published his letters in the local newspapers.

Moule explained that, since houses were in demand, rents were high. Even quite humble men, such as masons and carpenters, found it worth their while to run up cottages when other work was slack. For an outlay of £50 or less, and their labour, they could build a hovel and count on as much as £6 a year in rent. At a time when interest rates sometimes fell to 2%, this was an excellent return.

The usual plan for a cottage was one room downstairs, opening into the street, and one or two rooms upstairs. There was no other accommodation, not even a larder or coal house. A labourer's wages were unlikely to be higher than ten shillings a week, of which the rent took a quarter. Consequently, a family might have to take in lodgers, even though it had several children. There could be as many as nine people to a bedroom.

Moule described Fordington's sanitation:

> For twenty-three cottages, averaging six inhabitants to each, there are five 'conveniences' with only three vaults; in these vaults the water is within about four feet of the surface of the ground and

the wells from which the cottagers drink, are within ten or fifteen yards of them.

In a square of thirteen miserable cottages there cannot be said to be any 'convenience'; and on the other side, one is frequented by families numbering ninety, and another by those numbering more than one hundred men, women and children. The filth and vice can scarcely be conceived by anyone who has not almost daily descended from a high and pure atmosphere to live and breathe in this, and to observe what passes amongst people so circumstanced.

Once, when Moule was attending a dying man, there was a violent storm, so that a privy used by 13 families overflowed and its contents ran between him and the bed.

Disease was common. There was typhoid and typhus, both known from their main symptom as 'fever'. Smallpox, which had become a serious threat in the 18th century, continued its ravages. Chiefly a disease of the very young, it killed many and blinded and disfigured many more. There was also a new and terrifying danger, Asiatic cholera, which swept round the world in great pandemics. There were outbreaks at Dorchester in 1849 and 1854.

The visitation of 1854 came about because the Home Secretary, Lord Palmerston, decided that the best way to combat an epidemic in Mill Bank Penitentiary was to move the convicts into Dorchester's barracks. About 700 arrived and two Fordington women contracted to wash their bedding and garments. The women tipped their dirty water into the street, so that it ran between their neighbours' hovels on its way to the river. Shortly afterwards, cholera broke out along the trail of the soap suds. It was this which finally provoked Henry Moule's letters.

A method of preventing smallpox was at hand. In 1796 a Gloucestershire doctor called Edward Jenner proved by experiment that people were immune to smallpox, if vaccinated with the serum of a disease of cattle known as 'cowpox'. Jenner took the credit for this discovery, together with a reward of £30,000 from Parliament. But country folk had long been aware that those who had had cowpox did not catch smallpox. Some vaccinated themselves and others by introducing matter from a cowpox pustule into a scratch made by a needle. One such amateur doctor was a Yetminster farmer, Benjamin Jesty, who became more famous than the others because Jenner's enemies took him to London and made a fuss of him. In 1835 the vaccination of infants was made compulsory and smallpox declined.

Other diseases were more difficult to eradicate, partly because their causes were not understood and partly because such obvious measures as providing sewage works and pure water were expensive. There was also some apathy, because many diseases afflicted mainly the poor. Cholera, though, was no respecter of class, so when there was the threat of an epidemic in 1848, Parliament passed a Public Health Act. This created a new government department, the General Board of Health, and it also stated that any place which had a death rate higher than 23 per 1,000 had to elect its own Board of Health. Dorchester qualified.

Having a Board of Health did not guarantee that there would be any significant improvements. Dorchester's surveyor drew up a drainage scheme, but this was rejected as too expensive. It was cheaper and easier simply to instruct people to remove their 'nuisances'. The town had its first piped water as late as 1860 and had to wait for its sewage works until 1904.

Even though Dorset's towns were, to a certain extent, insanitary and poverty stricken, they at least kept some charm. Sir Frederick Treves describes Shaftesbury as he knew it at the turn of the century:

> In the morning the town wakes up. The householder opens his front door and stands out in the road in his shirt-sleeves to appraise the weather. The idle apprentice takes down the shop shutters, and – between intervals of gossip – places buckets, spades, tubs, horse-collars, and other goods, upon the pavement. The sexton strolls by to toll the morning bell. A leisurely man drags a drowsy horse to the blacksmith's to be shod, and in a while there is the sound of a hammer on an anvil. A passing gig, that started from some farmhouse at sunrise, interests the waking town. It may carry a dairymaid on her way to a new situation, a couple of milk cans, or a confused heifer under a net.
>
> A man proceeds to sweep the road with a besom made of a bundle of twigs according to the pattern of centuries ago. He shows a willingness to converse with everyone – man, woman or child – who will stop to 'pass the time of day with him.' As something of an event, a miller's cart, with a team of four fine horses, climbs up the High Street. There is always a vain, boastful dog with the waggon who clamours that the town should stir to see his horses, his wain, his waggoner, and his sacks, all of which he regards as of unequalled magnificence.
>
> In the evening the town goes lazily to sleep. The yawning shops close reluctantly, the long shadows of the setting sun fall across the drowsy street. The children have vanished. The lovers have come back from the lanes arm in arm. A tired dog is asleep in the centre

A small rural smithy in Dorset around the turn of the century. (Dorset County Museum)

of the road. Lights go out in the windows one by one, until the place is silent and dark.

The lot of the Dorset farm labourer did not improve during the Victorian period. Wages were no better than they had been in the days of the Tolpuddle Martyrs. In 1851, James Caird found that they were often only seven shillings a week and sometimes as low as six shillings. The lower amount would have been paid by a small farmer to an unmarried man. A wealthy employer might pay a good worker with a family as much as eleven shillings, but Caird's average of 8s 5d for the southern counties compares unfavourably with his figure of 11s 6d for the north of England. It was the industrial towns that accounted for the difference. They were islands of good wages which attracted people from the villages around them, so that farmers had to pay their workers reasonably well if they were to keep them. But in those days people were unwilling to move very far, so the influence of the towns rapidly diminished with the distance from them. Certainly, they had no effect on Dorset, where there was a surplus of labour. Here, women and children had to make up the earnings of the men.

The best paid employment for women and children was usually domestic crafts, such as button making, but there was work for them on the farms. From the age of twelve, girls picked potatoes and helped with the haymaking, though they were not strong enough to be of much value until they were about 14. They were often made to care for the younger children, so freeing their mothers for work. Boys might look after poultry, watch cattle and get in wood from the age of about seven, then go on to leading plough horses and helping with the harvest. From 13 they could hold the plough, help the carter, drive the team and clean out the stables. By the time they were 15 they were mowing, reaping, hedging and ditching.

As for the women, Mary Cox spoke for them all when she gave her evidence for the *Report on the Employment of Women and Children in Agriculture* of 1843:

> I am 35. I worked for Mr Ingram and then for Mr Fowler at Milton Abbas. I first went out to work when I was about 16 or 17. I have done harvest work, hay-making, couching, picking up stones, but no turnip hoeing or reaping. In harvest my work was tying up corn, which is the hardest kind of work. I have done all this kind of work since I first went out till now. I am married and have had several children. I never found the work hurt me. I used to make buttons before I went out to work in the fields. I was much better in health when working out of doors than when buttoning. I don't think there is anything wrong takes place in the harvest or hay field. Mr Ingram never allowed talking at those times. [*Harvest was, notoriously, a time for illicit sex.*]
>
> In the spring I used to work from eight till five; at hay-making from eight till sunset. I have always had 6d a day in the spring for weeding; 8d a day for hay-making; and 1s 0d a day for harvest. I don't think all women get 1s 0d a day at harvest, but I managed to work hard and earn it.

The same report describes a Dorset cottage:

> At Stourpaine, a village near Blandford, I measured a bedroom in a cottage consisting of two rooms, the bedroom in question upstairs,

Farm labourer's cottage. (Mansell Collection)

and a room on the ground floor in which the family lived during the day. There were eleven in the family. The bedroom was ten feet square, not reckoning the two small recesses by the side of the chimney, about 18 inches deep. The roof was of thatch, the middle of the chamber being about seven feet high. Opposite the fireplace was a small window, about 15 inches square, the only one to the room.

Bed A was occupied by the father and mother, a little boy, Jeremiah, aged $1\frac{1}{2}$ years, and an infant aged 4 months.

Bed B was occupied by the three daughters – the two eldest, Sarah and Elizabeth, twins, aged 20 and Mary, aged 7.

Bed C was occupied by the four sons – Silas, aged 17; John, aged 15; James, aged 14 and Elias, aged 10.

There was no curtain, or any kind of separation between the beds.

This description of Stourpaine had an interesting sequel. The landed interest had used its control of Parliament to impose duties on imported cereals by measures known as the Corn Laws. Industrialists objected, because this meant dear food for their employees, who demanded higher wages. The landed interest took its revenge by securing a series of official inquiries into the evils of the factories and the factory towns. One of the critics who was most vociferous and who adopted a high moral tone, was that great reformer Lord Ashley, eldest son of the sixth Earl of Shaftesbury. To the delight of the opponents of the Corn Laws, it emerged that the Stourpaine hovel was on the Shaftesbury estates. For a brief space, it was nationally famous.

Conditions in the Dorset countryside became even worse with the agricultural depression of the last quarter of the century. Many labourers could stand no more, so they left. Some went to other parts of Britain, while others emigrated to various parts of the Empire, benevolent clergy and landowners often paying their passages. One contingent even went to Brazil. There were not enough emigrants to bring about a decline in the population, but there was at least a check to its growth.

We can see the results of these changes from Sir Frederick Treves's description of Cerne Abbas at the turn of the century:

> The place is empty and decaying and strangely silent. Grass is growing in the streets; many houses have been long deserted, many have their windows boarded up, or are falling into listless ruin. Here are empty barns, gates falling off their hinges, and doorways grown up with weeds. There are quaint old shops with bow windows, but the windows are empty of everything but a faded red curtain, while over the door, in very dim paint, are traces of a name. One feels compelled to walk very quietly through the echoing streets, and to talk in whispers, for fear that the sleep of Cerne should be broken.

The Dorset farm labourers found a champion in the Rev Lord Sidney Godolphin Osborne, third son of the Duke of Leeds, and rector of Durweston from 1841 to 1875. A garrulous man, Osborne wrote incessantly to *The Times* on anything from free trade to cattle plague. One of his favourite topics, though, was the plight of the Dorset labourers, which he described vividly. But the only practical help Osborne gave was to pay the passages of a few emigrants. His colleague Huxtable did more by creating employment on his efficient farms. It should be mentioned, though, that the young Charles Kingsley lived with the Osbornes for the short time that he was a curate at Pimperne, and the Rev Lord Sidney did much to turn his thoughts to social reform.

At this time, Dorset produced one of Britain's best known reformers. He was Anthony Ashley Cooper, the Lord Ashley who was to become the seventh Earl of Shaftesbury. He had been so strident in his criticisms of the factory and mine owners that when he inherited his 18,000 acres in 1851 he had no choice but to make some improvements. Farms

A steam threshing engine at work in a Dorset field at the turn of the century. (Dorset County Museum)

were consolidated, some decent cottages were built and there was an ambitious scheme of land drainage. For this, Shaftesbury borrowed £32,000, hoping he could recoup his money by increasing rents when the work was finished, and that in the meantime there would be employment for many of the labourers on his estates. Shaftesbury, though, lacked the skill and the application to carry through his scheme, so he returned to London where he devoted himself to 'the factory children, the chimney sweeps, the milliners, the Druses of Syria and the Italians oppressed under alien rule.'

Management of the estates was now in the hands of Shaftesbury's agent, Robert Short Waters. With £21,000 a year passing through his hands, the only accounts Waters kept were jottings in his diary. He was, moreover, dishonest, among other things conspiring with the drainage contractors to rob his employer. The work was done so badly

Bronze of Thomas Hardy, Dorchester, by Eric Kennington.

that there was no improvement to the fields and the farmers objected to the increased rents.

Eventually, Shaftesbury's father-in-law, Lord Palmerston, became suspicious of Waters, and all sorts of malpractices came to light. Shaftesbury sued Waters in Chancery and Waters, believing attack was the best form of defence, counter-sued Shaftesbury. In the end, both parties agreed to abandon their suits, leaving Shaftesbury with an enormous legal bill and complaining that, 'Our blessed Saviour knew every affliction save that of being in debt.'

Mention must be made of two Dorset writers, both of whom have their statues in Dorchester. One was William Barnes (1801–1886), who wrote poetry in the Dorset dialect. Thanks, partly, to Barnes, preserving the dialect became an obsession with numbers of people, though they would never have allowed their own children to speak it.

The other writer was Thomas Hardy (1840–1928), author of the famous Wessex novels. Hardy has his loyal readers, who explore the countryside that he describes so vividly, eager to identify places mentioned in the novels. On the other hand, there are many who reject Hardy's works as too morbid. Laughter, he said, 'always means blindness, either from defect, choice or accident.'

22

BOURNEMOUTH
A VICTORIAN PRODIGY

During Queen Victoria's reign, Bournemouth grew from practically nothing into a flourishing county borough. It was an astonishing development and one of national importance.

For centuries, the land on which Bournemouth now stands attracted few settlements, for it was a barren heath. Then, during the Napoleonic Wars, Captain Lewis Tregonwell was stationed on the shores of Poole Bay and he decided that a site near the mouth of the little river Bourne would be just the place for his summer residence. He bought eight acres of land and by 1812 had finished his house which he called 'The Mansion'. In 1820, he let it to the Marchioness of Exeter for the season, and thereafter it was known as Exeter House. Today, it is part of the Exeter Hotel. Tregonwell also built some cottages which he let during the summer.

Tregonwell died in 1832, but when Sir George William Tapps-Gervis inherited the manor of Christchurch in 1835, he decided to make Bournemouth a 'watering place for the genteel elderly.' He planted numerous pines and built Westover Villas, Westover Gardens and the Bath Hotel. The hotel was finished in 1838, in time to open on the day of Queen Victoria's coronation.

Doctors helped the growth of the new resort. Dr A. Granville in his 1841 edition of the *Spas of England* said the place was 'ideal for a convalescent free from positive disease, but also for patients in the most delicate state of health as to lungs and for the wealthy afflicted with disease.' Dr Aitken of Poole analysed the waters of the Bourne and pronounced them free from dung.

Later in the century, Dr Horace Dobell was impressed by the cure he found at Mont Dore in the Auvergne and decided to practise it in Bournemouth, where the pines gave off what he thought was a healthy aroma. In 1885 he built the ugly Mont Dore Hotel, imported water from the Auvergne and began giving treatment.

By 1851 the population of Bournemouth was 605, and it soared to

Lewis Tregonwell, founder of Bournemouth (Dorset County Library).

16,859 in 1881 and 59,762 in 1901. At the same time, the town improved its status. In 1856 it secured an Improvement Act, putting it in charge of 13 commissioners. Two were the lord of the manor and his nominee, while the remainder were elected by ratepayers occupying property to the value of £30 a year. The commissioners were empowered to pave the streets, provide sewers, drainage, lighting and cleansing and build a pier. The town became a municipal borough in 1890 and a county borough in 1900. Over the years, it also extended its boundaries. Its misfortune was to be born just when good taste in architecture had died so that, apart from some of the churches, it has no buildings of merit.

Bournemouth was well provided with places of worship. When Alexander Morton Bennett was appointed vicar in 1845, a church was being built on the site now occupied by St Peter's. It was not good enough for him, so, in 1853, he appointed G. E. Street to provide something grander. St Peter's was ready for worship in 1858 and by 1879 had acquired a tower and a spire. Bennett was a Tractarian, so he displeased the Evangelicals in the town, who built Holy Trinity as a rival to St Peter's. When Morton Bennett died in 1880, St Stephen's was built in his memory, at a cost of £30,000. Bennett's son, who became the first vicar, was even more High Church than his father.

Morton Bennett kept a close eye on the settlements growing up around Bournemouth, making sure they had the churches and schools they needed. He was responsible for finding no less than eight sites.

There were a good many Nonconformists in the town. The Congregationalists built a chapel in Orchard Street in 1849, and then a larger one on Richmond Hill in 1891. Here, holidaymakers queued to hear the sermons of Dr J. D. Jones, known as 'Jones of Bournemouth'. The Beale and Bright families, the town's leading shopkeepers, attended this church. The Presbyterians had an iron church in 1857, a stone one in

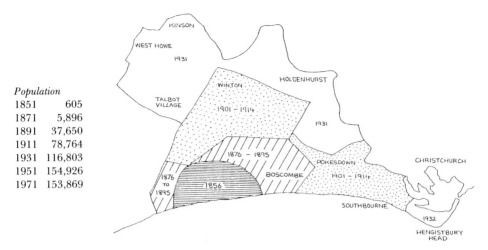

Population

1851	605
1871	5,896
1891	37,650
1911	78,764
1931	116,803
1951	154,926
1971	153,869

Growth of Bournemouth.

1872 and moved to their present chapel in Exeter Road in 1888. The Baptists built a chapel on the Lansdowne in 1876. The Methodists began by meeting in a rented room, but they had a chapel on Richmond Hill by 1886, which they called the Punshon Memorial Church, after one of their outstanding preachers, the Rev Dr W. Morley Punshon. A German bomb demolished this building in 1943, and it was replaced by another in Exeter Road which was dedicated in 1958. This was the first of Bournemouth's churches to escape from the mock-Gothic. The architect, Ronald Sims, was awarded the bronze medal of the Royal Institute of British Architects for his work, but Pevsner describes its slender spire as 'a tall spike' and adds that the building, 'is spiky also in other ways typical of church designing today.'

The Roman Catholics built their first public chapel in 1869, which was followed by the Oratory of the Sacred Heart and Corpus Christi. In 1870, the nuns of the Congregation of the Cross arrived from St Quentin. They built the Convent of St Joseph, with a school attached.

Jews arrived in about 1900, opened three boarding houses for their own people in 1905 and built a synagogue in 1910.

Churchmen saw it as their duty to provide schools and there was money enough in Bournemouth to do this. Most were National Schools, beginning with St Peter's in 1840, but the Nonconformists opened a British School in 1858 and the Catholics had a school by 1877. There was never any danger of a School Board. Being a new town, Bournemouth had no ancient endowed grammar school, but the Municipal Grammar and Technical School for Boys opened in Porchester Road in 1901. There were the beginnings of higher education as well, for three

187

The pier approach, Bournemouth, 1890. (Dorset County Library)

technical schools opened in 1889 and they amalgamated to form the Municipal College on the Lansdowne in 1913.

Shops soon made their appearance, one announcing that 'mourning clothes could be provided at short notice.' Later, Frederick Bright, a retired missionary, opened a needlework shop, while a lay preacher, John Elmes Beale, opened a drapery he called 'Fancy Fair'. Both establishments were to grow into large department stores. Henry Joy built the Arcade, known as 'Joy's Folly', between 1866 and 1873, at the same time destroying a beauty spot called Church Glen.

The town developed a good system of public transport, which began modestly enough with horse buses running to Poole. In 1880 the Royal Blue Coach Operators started a service to Holmsley, which was Christchurch's station on 'Castleman's Corkscrew', and after 1911 the company was using motor buses. In the town itself there were horse omnibuses from the 1880s and by 1899, eight-seater motor wagonettes were travelling between Pokesdown and Westbourne. In 1901 the Poole and District Electric Traction Company laid its tramlines as far as County Gates, but, for a time, Bournemouth would let them go no further. It soon changed its mind, though, and after 1903 there were trams running through the town from Poole to Christchurch.

There were determined efforts to make Bournemouth attractive. Following the Improvement Act of 1856, the Commissioners drained the land either side of the Bourne and created the gardens which, more than anything, give the town charm and character. The act of 1856 also empowered the Commissioners to build a pier, which they did in 1861.

Pleasure steamers used it, running a regular service to Swanage and excursions to the Isle of Wight, the Channel Islands and to France. In those days, no passports were needed. The wooden pier suffered from storms and toredo worms, so in 1880 it was replaced with an iron one which was, eventually, 1,000 feet long. The Winter Gardens pavilion was built in 1876, a large, iron-framed glasshouse containing exotic plants. In 1907, the undercliff drive was finished as far as Meyrick Road, with zig-zag paths linking it to the cliff tops. Eventually, it joined Bournemouth and Boscombe piers.

In 1893 Dan Godfrey formed an orchestra of 30 musicians, and that same year his father, also called Dan, brought the band of the Grenadier Guards to give a joint performance. It was a huge success. By 1895 the orchestra was performing not only military music, but Beethoven and Mozart as well. The town council took over the orchestra in 1896, making it the first in Britain to be run by a municipality. The Winter Gardens had been a failure, so the building became the orchestra's home. The musicians called it the 'cucumber frame'. The acoustics were poor and when heavy rain drummed on the roof, it killed the music. Godfrey was given the title of 'Musical Director and General Manager of the Winter Gardens'. Having succeeded with the great classical masters he thought it safe to proceed to chamber music and then to the works of his favourites, contemporary English composers such as Holst, Parry and Elgar. His aim, he said, was to 'foster musical education and appreciation.' Giving his audiences what he thought might be good for them, rather than what they would enjoy, meant that the orchestra lost money.

An important issue in the latter part of the 19th century was whether Bournemouth should remain somewhat exclusive, a place where the genteel came to convalesce, retire and die, or whether it should become a popular resort. There was no doubt what the genteel themselves wanted, and many shopkeepers supported them, for they wanted to keep their high spending customers. One way to ensure the town remained select was to prevent the building of a railway.

The railway, though, insinuated itself gradually. Bournemouth East Station finally opened in 1870, after which every bank holiday saw increasing numbers of relatively humble folk from London and Birmingham buying their excursion tickets at five shillings each, and arriving for a day by the sea. They crowded the beach, where there were games, swings, rowing boats, donkeys, and Punch and Judy shows. Many enjoyed sea bathing, in spite of the strict rules. Apart from one or two small areas, there were separate sections of the beach for men and women.

As well as the crowds, Bournemouth had its share of famous visitors and residents. Disraeli once held a cabinet meeting in the Bath Hotel. Gladstone took his last communion in St Peter's church. Charles Darwin made a short stay, complaining, 'The country is like Patagonia.' Sir Percy Shelley, the son of the poet, bought Boscombe Manor, and created a cultural centre with a theatre that would seat 300. Robert Louis Stevenson hoped the sea air and the pines might cure his tuberculosis, so he took a house in Alum Chine Road, Westbourne; it was here that he wrote *The Strange Case of Dr Jekyll and Mr Hyde*. Marconi operated one of his early radio stations from the Madeira Hotel in Southcliff Road. Winston Churchill was brought here, when a boy. While playing a game of chase with some friends, he tried to escape by jumping off the suspension bridge in Alum Chine. He missed the branch he had hoped to catch, and was lucky to survive. Charles Rolls, of Rolls-Royce, did manage to kill himself, in an aeroplane crash. But perhaps the most interesting visitor of all was Emilie Charlotte le Breton, otherwise known as Lillie Langtry, the mistress of Edward, Prince of Wales. Edward built a home for her known as the Red House. On the minstrels' gallery was the motto, 'They say – What say they? Let them say!'

Bournemouth's most famous citizen was perhaps Merton Russell-Coates. In 1876 he bought the Bath Hotel, which he renamed the 'Royal Bath'. He had travelled widely, making a remarkable collection of works of art from all over the world. At first, he exhibited his treasures in the hotel, but then he built East Cliff Hall to house them, and as a home for his wife.

Russell-Coates involved himself in the life of the town. Among other things he advised the building of a 'fever hospital', which was an unfortunate choice of name, and he was burnt in effigy. He had what he wanted in the end, but with the more innocent title of 'sanitary hospital'. It later became part of the Royal Victoria Hospital. In 1890, when the town became a municipal borough, Russell-Coates presented it with a mace and a mayoral badge. He became mayor himself in 1894. He gave his vigorous support to the building of the undercliff drive, which, as we have seen, opened as far as Meyrick Road in 1907. To celebrate the event, he and his wife presented East Cliff Hall and its contents to the town. It is now the Russell-Coates Art Gallery and Museum.

As Bournemouth was growing, other settlements appeared in its neighbourhood, all of them eventually merging to form one conurbation.

Boscombe in 1850 consisted of little more than a pub called the Ragged Cat, a few cottages and Sir Percy Shelley's Boscombe Manor. Soon, rows of terraced houses were built for workmen who were employed in Bournemouth, but Sir Henry Drummond had higher ambitions for the place. He built Boscombe Towers and then the Boscombe Spa Hotel, hoping to exploit a small spring whose waters, so he thought, had healing properties. Bournemouth's zealous vicar, Alexander Morton Bennett, raised money to buy a site for a church, and Edmund Christy gave £30,000 for the building. It was consecrated as St Clement's in 1873. The ritual was High Church, which did not suit the people of the parish, so they burnt Morton Bennett in effigy. A pier was built in 1889 and then an arcade and a theatre, all in the vain hope of rivalling Bournemouth.

At Southbourne, Dr Thomas Compton bought 230 acres of land with a mile of sea front, intending to found a health resort. Like Tregonwell at Bournemouth and Drummond at Boscombe, he arrived, was enchanted by the area and then proceeded to spoil it by building on it. Southbourne acquired a winter gardens pavilion, brought from Andover, a church, an iron pier and an undercliff esplanade. A storm destroyed both pier and esplanade in 1907.

Some of the inland settlements like Winton and Pokesdown were, for the most part, working class suburbs. Others were inhabited by the wealthy who built enormous detached villas, described by William Morris as fit only for 'ignorant, purse-proud digesting machines'. Talbot Village has a history of some interest. It began when two spinster ladies called Georgina and Marianne Talbot moved to a house on the East Cliff in Bournemouth, where they were sometimes besieged by hungry people demanding work. Rather than give charity, they bought some land to the north of the town where they built a number of decent cottages, each with an acre of ground. The tenants were expected to make a living for themselves by keeping pigs and poultry. The sisters also built almshouses, a school and, of course, a church. Georgina was the first to be buried in its graveyard. The inscription on her Memorial Cross reads:

In the neighbourhood of this village she passed 25 years of blameless life giving up time and fortune to bettering the conditions of the poorer classes, seeking to minister to their temporal and spiritual welfare, and erecting habitations suitable to their position in life, herself enjoying a peaceful and happy existence in doing good, waiting for the end.

23

THE TWENTIETH CENTURY

In the early years of the 20th century, life went on as before for most of the people of Dorset. There were, though miscellaneous events and developments which hinted at the changes to come, but few would have realised their significance at the time.

In 1897, Russian emigrants led by Vladimir Tchertkoff arrived in Tuckton, where they established the Free Age Press and printed the works of Tolstoy that were forbidden in their own country. This was a step, if only a very small one, towards the Russian revolutions of 1905 and 1917.

Kaiser William II was a frequent visitor to the Bournemouth area. In 1908 he was staying at Highcliffe Castle, where he gave an interview to a reporter from *The Daily Telegraph*. During it, he said that in Germany there was growing hostility towards Britain, though, for his own part, he was doing his best to combat it. This tactless remark worsened relations between the two countries and hastened the slide to war.

There were two events of scientific importance. In 1897 Marconi set up a wireless mast outside the Haven Hotel, Sandbanks, and worked in a room in the hotel for many years. In 1910, Charles Rolls of Rolls-Royce killed himself in a flying accident near Hengistbury Head, so adding, unintentionally and tragically, to the sum of experience needed for the development of aviation.

There was a small but important development in tourism. Large numbers of trippers and holidaymakers were already coming to the resorts by train and some extended their journeys by steamer, though they could only do so to other coastal towns. Now, they were able to roam inland in hideously uncomfortable, open topped charabancs, the precursors of the modern coach. Sir Frederick Treves described the tea garden at Sutton Poyntz, 'where char-à-bancs from Weymouth, for the fee of one shilling each, bring hundreds of hearty folk, who clamour for "shrimp and lobster teas", pelt the ducks in the pond and "rot" dignified villagers with unintelligible jests.'

This was also the golden age of Brownsea Island. It had been, on the whole, unlucky in its owners. In the 18th century they included William Benson, Wren's successor as Surveyor of Works. Benson practised black magic, dancing naked round a fire, and, according to legend, the island echoed one night to the screams of a servant girl he was sacrificing. In the 1850s, Colonel William Waugh tried to establish a porcelain factory on the island, believing it contained large deposits of china clay. He was wrong, and, having discovered his mistake, he absconded to Spain, leaving massive debts. However, in 1901 a wealthy Dutchman called Charles van Raalte bought Brownsea, and made it quite a centre of society, with a constant stream of distinguished guests, including minor royalty. There was an estate band of 22 musicians which played at the many dances and parties. The van Raaltes were also good to their employees; for example, they entertained the entire population of the island to Christmas lunch.

It was Charles van Raalte who gave Brownsea its present name. Formerly it was 'Branksea', but he changed it because so many of his visitors left the train at Branksome station, instead of going on to Poole. When van Raalte died in 1908, his widow tried to continue as before, but she lost much of her money in unwise investments, including a project to build ships from concrete.

In 1907 van Raalte had allowed Baden-Powell to hold his first, experimental camp on Brownsea. Some 20 boys from different backgrounds attended. Baden-Powell judged his experiment to be a success and, the following year, he founded the Boy Scout movement, with himself as Chief Scout. In 1910 the Girl Guides followed, Baden-Powell's wife, Olave, becoming Chief Guide in 1918. Olave had been born in Lilliput, and the couple were married in St Peter's church, Parkstone.

Baden-Powell won fame as the defender of Mafeking during the Boer War, but if the Boers failed to take the town it was because, for most of the time, they did not even try. Later, when Baden-Powell commanded a force in the field, he showed that he was incompetent, neglecting even the basic principle of 'marching towards the sound of the guns'. Worse, his treatment of the black people in his care at Mafeking was brutal. There is an account of his military career in Thomas Pakenham's scholarly work, *The Boer War*.

The 20th century had hardly begun, when the possibility of war with Germany began to loom. During Victoria's reign, the British had kept their fleet at the 'two power standard', that is, as strong as any two navies in the world combined. As a result, they felt immune from attack and followed a policy of 'splendid isolation'. The Boer War of 1899–1902 destroyed this complacency, for a handful of South African farmers not only challenged the British Empire, but nearly defeated it. The

British were also thoroughly alarmed when Germany began building a large, modern navy. The Kaiser made soothing noises, saying it was 'for Germany', not 'against Britain', but he failed to reassure. If the country with the most powerful army in Europe also acquired the most powerful navy, then Britain would be at her mercy. The result was a naval race, during which both sides built numbers of hugely expensive but largely ineffective battleships, known as 'Dreadnoughts'.

For Dorset, the German threat meant that the Portland naval base became much more important. As we have seen, the breakwater was begun in 1849, to be followed by the two fortresses of the Nothe and the Verne. In the 20th century, there seemed to be three dangers. One was from torpedo boats. It was feared that these fast moving little craft might cause havoc among the great ships of the Royal Navy as they lay at anchor. Accordingly, two extra breakwaters were built at Portland, to enclose the harbour completely, and in 1914, an old battleship, HMS *Hood*, was sunk in the South Ship Channel, leaving only the North and East Ship Channels to be defended. Another threat was that a hostile fleet might appear off the base, so six howitzers were mounted near the Verne, whose role was to deliver plunging fire on the decks of enemy warships, where their armour was weakest. The third menace was submarines. Fortunately, by the time the Germans began unrestricted U-boat warfare in 1917, there were the means of combating it, such as detection devices and depth charges.

Apart from shortages and rationing, civilians in Dorset had little to endure during the First World War, but there was a ceaseless flow of telegrams bringing news of deaths at the front. Every town and village has its war memorial, with a long list of names.

In the fighting, the Dorset Regiment was the first British unit to suffer a gas attack, and there were heavy losses in all the great battles, while in 1916 the Dorset Yeomanry Cavalry proved to the satisfaction of the High Command, at least, that 'it was possible for determined horsemen to ride through machine-gun fire in action.' The Second Dorsets were part of Allenby's army, which drove the Turks out of Palestine.

Dorset had two other, more tenuous, links with Palestine. In 1916, the Royal Navy acquired, at Churchill's insistence, its own cordite factory. This was on Holton Heath, near Wareham. The manufacture of cordite required acetone, so a second factory was built on the heath to supply it. The scientist in charge was a Russo-Polish Jew called Chaim Weizmann, who had developed a fermentation process that produced some 20,000 tons of acetone before the end of the war. Weizmann, therefore, played a key part in the defeat of the U-boats and his success gave him the ear of Britain's leading politicians. He was one of the leaders of the

Zionist movement, and used his influence on its behalf. In 1917, the British government issued what is known as the 'Balfour Declaration', promising the Jews a national home in Palestine.

At the same time, the British were encouraging the Arabs of the Middle East to rebel against their Turkish masters by agreeing to work for their freedom. This promise included, of course, the Arabs of Palestine. Directing many of the Arabs' operations was the remarkable T. E. Lawrence, 'of Arabia'. After the war, he felt his Arab friends had been betrayed, so he sent back his medals and tried to secure anonymity by vanishing into the ranks of the Services. In 1925 he bought the cottage of Clouds Hill, near Wareham. Ten years later, 'Aircraftsman Shaw' died in a motorcycling accident on a Dorset road.

After the First World War there was a brief economic boom, which was followed by stagnation and then, in the 1930s, by a depression so severe that it has passed into folk memory.

Farming had been in decline since the 1870s, and though it revived during the war because of the U-boats, peace brought ever increasing imports of food from the Empire and from Denmark. The government did a little to help, for example by creating Marketing Boards for potatoes, milk and pigs. Mainly, though, it was concerned to find markets for British industrial goods and at the Ottawa Conference in 1932 Britain agreed not to impose duties on food from the Commonwealth countries, while, for their part, they agreed they would not impose duties on British manufactures. In Britain, the only farming activity likely to make a profit was dairying, since it was impossible to import fresh milk.

As food prices fell, so did rents and land values. Moreover, the wealthy were, for the first time, having to pay considerable death duties. Once a sacred possession, land had become a liability, and many owners decided they must sell. To give just three examples from 1919, the Godmanstone estate parted with 1,100 acres, the Osmington estate with 2,000 acres and the Kingston Lacy and Corfe Castle estates with 2,600 acres. Sales like this were happening all over the country, and the result was the most massive transfer of land that had taken place in England since the dissolution of the monasteries. Most of the purchasers were the sitting tenants. In Dorset, they paid £14 an acre or less, but, in general, they made bad bargains. Abbey Farm at Cerne Abbas sold for £7,600 in 1919 and £6,350 in 1937, a loss of 16%. Also, the new owners found that the banks and building societies that had advanced the purchase money were much less tolerant of late payment than their former landlords had been.

During the great depression, it was the industrial towns on the coalfields that suffered the most. Dorset had no such towns, and

195

so escaped the worst of the troubles. In the late 1930s a modest building boom began to lead Britain out of the depression, and Dorset's brickyards thrived. As for Poole Pottery, it flourished throughout. In 1921, John Adams became its managing director. Himself a gifted artist, he gathered a team of brilliant designers and craftsmen and craftswomen. Their goods were exported all over the world.

Civic improvement continued. Poole Council had already taken over the town's water works in 1906 and, in 1922, it opened a sewage farm at Fleetsbridge. In 1925 the town was given a new gas works. It was at Pitwines, a site for which there was assuredly a better use, since it adjoins Baiter, which commands superb views of the harbour and the Isle of Purbeck. The huge gasometer dominated the skyline, while fumes and dust from the retorts spread over the neighbourhood.

One method of combating the depression was to create employment with public works. In the United States, President Roosevelt led the way with his 'New Deal', and though the British government was more cautious it did try the same policy. Among other things, it gave Poole a substantial grant towards the cost of the handsome new Municipal Buildings. They may be seen as Dorset's equivalent of the Hoover Dam. At the same time, Poole Secondary School received some new classrooms, though they were built as cheaply as possible and safety officers were to denounce them repeatedly as a serious fire hazard.

An increase in the number of motor cars brought the demise of the tram. Many cars had narrow tyres, so their drivers needed to master complicated drills for extracting themselves from tram lines, should they be careless enough to drive into them. Even worse was the tram's inability to pull into the kerb when it stopped. The last tram in the Poole and Bournemouth area ran in 1935. Perversely, the two places adopted different alternatives, Bournemouth having trolley buses, and Poole, motor buses.

Brownsea Island went through a depression of its own, for in 1927 Mary Florence Bonham-Cox-Christie bought it, in order to live on it as a recluse. She gave her agent one year to expel the inhabitants. A paralysed man who hung on to the last was ejected from his home and his belongings were dumped on the beach. Cattle were left to wander unattended until they died of disease and starvation, the cows also suffering agony from not being milked. If anyone was so foolish as to land, Christie's female Swedish bouncer flung them into the sea. Meanwhile, the island became an overgrown wilderness. In 1934, there was a fire. The Poole brigade arrived and Christie did not order it to leave, but it could do little since its hoses were the wrong size for the antiquated hydrants. The fire burnt for a week, killing many animals.

Christie lived to be 98 and when she died in 1961, her grandson and heir announced that in conformity with her wishes, he was going to leave Brownsea exactly as it was. He had, though, to part with it in order to meet death duties and, eventually, it passed to the National Trust.

Between the wars, the foreign policies of Britain and France were confused, partly because they could not decide whether communism or fascism was the greater threat, and partly because they were engrossed in domestic problems. Meanwhile, Hitler went from strength to strength.

In 1938, events moved quickly. First, Austria was united to Germany, and then Hitler demanded the Sudentenland, the border country of Czechoslovakia, where there were German minorities, as well as a mountain barrier with powerful defences. There followed the Munich agreement, whereby Chamberlain of Britain and Daladier of France agreed that they would compel Czechoslovakia to surrender the territory, in return for a promise of 'peace in our time'. This was Chamberlain's famous 'piece of paper', which he flaunted with pride when he returned to Britain. Such was the policy of 'appeasement'.

Many British people were aghast at the betrayal of Czechoslovakia and even some politicians were critical. Chief among them was Winston Churchill, but there was also Viscount Cranborne, MP for South Dorset. After Munich, he resigned as Under Secretary for Foreign Affairs and stumped round his constituency, uttering warnings.

At the beginning of the Second World War there was a blackout, which led to road accidents, and drunks stumbling into Weymouth Harbour, where they drowned. Gas masks were issued, their owners happily unaware that they would be quite ineffective against the Germans' new nerve gases. Volunteers filled sandbags to protect public buildings, though most had had enough after one day. Droves of evacuees arrived. Some made lifelong friendships with local people, but many wet their beds, quarrelled with their hosts and returned home, leaving behind debts and vivid impressions of life in the slums of the East End. Ration books were issued, which led to a thriving Black Market. The Earl of Shaftesbbury, Lord Lieutenant of Dorset, and his son, Viscount Cranborne, were both convicted of buying butter illegally.

The fall of France in June 1940 meant that the Germans were only 70 miles away, in the Cherbourg peninsula. Dorset was now in the front line. The first sign of this was the arrival of battle worn British and French soldiers, evacuated from Dunkirk. Dorset's pleasure steamers went to help with 'Operation Dynamo', for which they were ideal, since carrying trippers on the English Channel was their function. They picked up the troops on the mole at Dunkirk, from where most of them escaped not, as is sometimes believed, from the beaches. Dorset fishermen went to help as well, but the Admiralty rejected their offers, commandeered their boats and sent them home by train.

Refugees also arrived, some from Holland, Belgium and France, but most from the Channel Islands. Over 27,000 poured through Weymouth in a single week.

The next stage of the war was the Battle of Britain, and two squadrons of Spitfires came to Warmwell. They fought bravely, if not always with great success, for their enemies were more experienced. Luckily, the Messerschmitts could not carry enough fuel for a sustained battle far from base.

During and after the Battle of Britain there were numerous air raids. At first Poole and Christchurch suffered the most, but on 30th September 1940, German bombers dropped 300 bombs on Sherborne in three minutes, killing 17 people, putting 32 in hospital and destroying or damaging 766 of the town's 1,700 houses.

Following its defeat in the daylight skies, the Luftwaffe bombed at night. A raid on Bournemouth in May 1943 killed 77 people and damaged nearly 3,500 buildings. To guide the bombers, pathfinder aircraft would arrive first to drop incendiary bombs and to counter this, the British developed the 'Starfish' apparatus, which created the same effect as incendiaries. In May 1942, Starfish led the Germans to drop 1,000 tons of bombs on Brownsea Island, instead of Poole and Bournemouth. In June, a decoy at Arne saved the Royal Navy Cordite Factory on Holton Heath. Later the same month, the Germans created their own decoy by setting fire to the heath near Hamworthy.

There was plenty of action in the Channel, where ships were sunk by submarines, mines, E-boats and Stuka dive bombers. The Stukas had their first success in July 1940, when they sank HMS *Foylebank*, an anti-aircraft auxiliary, in Portland Harbour. Occasionally, enemy craft came close enough for the shore batteries to engage them.

Civilians did what they could. They 'dug for victory', joined the Home Guard and the Women's Land Army and raised money. The cruiser HMS *Dorsetshire* fired the last shots which sank the *Bismarck*, but in April 1942 she was herself sunk by the Japanese. The county set itself the target of £2.75 million to replace her and raised over £3 million.

There were defences along the Dorset coast, especially in Poole Bay where it would have been easy for the enemy to land. Here, the army dug trenches, put up barbed wire and removed the beach huts to improve the field of fire. One scheme was 'Sea-flame', by which oil would have been pumped on the sea and then set alight when enemy landing craft reached it. Tests soon proved that this would work only in a flat calm.

In December 1941, Japan attacked Pearl Harbour, forcing the United

States to declare war. American troops began arriving in Britain and the long preparations for an invasion of France began. Dorset provided many of the weapons. The Royal Navy Cordite Factory produced explosives, J. Bolson and Son of Hamworthy built landing craft and the Airspeed factory at Christchurch made gliders.

Dorset was also a training ground and a base for operations. The army extended its Lulworth ranges, which meant evicting the people of Tynham from their homes. The Americans and the British rehearsed landings on Studland beach and Brownsea Island. PLUTO, the oil pipe line, was run from Poole to the Isle of Wight, for testing. Massive quantities of stores and huge numbers of vehicles were assembled. American Lightnings operated from Warmwell, while Blandford Camp became a US army hospital.

Until 1944 there was no warship larger than a destroyer based on Portland, for the navy's capital ships had been sent to the far north, to save them from the Luftwaffe. Then, in June 1944, the huge battleship HMS *Rodney* arrived in Portland harbour, so that she could help with the invasion of France. The one effective use of such costly, vulnerable leviathans was to bombard coastal defences.

On D-Day, 6th June 1944, Halifax tug planes towed the gliders of the British 6th Airborne Division from Tarrant Rushton to France and 300 craft sailed from Poole Harbour, but the biggest exodus was from Weymouth and Portland Harbours. Here, 517,816 troops and 144,093 vehicles embarked during the eleven months between the invasion of France and the end of the war.

The people of Tynham had been as good as promised that they could return to their homes after the war, but Attlee's government refused permission and the village is still deserted. Crichel Down had been an RAF bombing range, but since it was no longer in use its owner, Lieut-Commander Marten, requested its return. He was rebuffed by an insolent bureaucrat. That led to the 'Battle of Crichel Down' which ended in victory for Commander Marten and the resignation of the Minister of Agriculture.

During the latter half of the 20th century, Britain went through a second industrial revolution, and it was based not on coal but electricity. That meant Dorset, like the rest of southern England, was able to play a full part in it. New, light industries appeared, most of them far more profitable than the traditional heavy industries of the coalfields.

Many of the factories were on the outskirts of Poole and Bournemouth. Hamworthy Engineering began modestly enough, but it expanded rapidly and increased its range of products. Other companies were Max Factor, Ryvita, British Drug Houses, Metal Box and Loewy

Robertson, with Flight Refuelling not far away at Wimborne. There were also numerous small firms that were, collectively, important. As yachting became more and more popular, boat building flourished. A later development, partly the result of high office rents in London, was the arrival of important commercial organisations, such as Barclays International, Chase Manhattan and Abbey Life.

There was also a new extractive industry, drilling for oil though it hardly benefits the local economy. Prospectors found small quantities of oil at Kimmeridge in 1959, and then, in 1974, significant amounts at Wytch Farm in Purbeck. This became the most productive on-shore field in Britain. The oil extends under Poole Harbour and well out to sea. Though BP was allowed to drill on Furzey Island, there was no question of a permanent rig in Poole Bay. The company proposed an artificial island, but the government, under pressure from the local MPs, refused permission. This was just before the general election of 1992, and the Conservatives could not afford to lose a single constituency.

Meanwhile, traditional industries survived. Tourism remained important. Holidays with pay and higher wages meant that soon after the war there were large numbers of summer visitors. Many stayed in the new caravan parks. These did little for the landscape, but they allowed large numbers of ordinary folk to enjoy seaside holidays which they could not otherwise have afforded. Later, there was competition from the Mediterranean resorts, but Poole Harbour is ideal for yachts and remained popular with their owners. In the harbour during the late 1980s, there were at any one time as many as 4,000 yachts on swinging moorings and 4,000 more in marinas.

Purbeck and Portland stone were still quarried, while there was much more demand for ball clay, which found many new uses, such as crucibles, and insulators to carry high voltage electricity cables. The manufacture of coarse pottery, like drain pipes, declined in the east of the county as the clay was exhausted, but Poole Pottery still thrived, exporting many of its products and acting as a tourist attraction. At Bridport, the rope and net industry showed it was still able to adapt, using new materials, artificial fibres, and new machines that could tie 30,000 million knots a year. Firms amalgamated until Bridport-Gundry was the only one.

During the war, BOAC flying boats used Poole Harbour as a base for services to West Africa, India, the Far East and Australia. Flights continued until the harbour was needed for the D-Day preparations and, though they resumed after the war, the flying boats soon returned to their original base at Hythe. However, RAF Hurn, which had been opened in 1941, became Bournemouth International Airport.

Barclays International, Poole.

Conventional trade through the port of Poole tended to decline in the 1970s, but in 1972 a French owned company called Truckline was formed to run a ferry for lorries and production cars between Poole and Cherbourg. It will be remembered that the plan to link the two towns in the 1860s had come to nothing, but Truckline was an immediate success. The service grew rapidly, so that in the year 1987/8 it carried 75,000 lorries and 20,000 cars. Measured by the tonnage of its trade in 1988, Poole came 21st in the order of British ports, while measured by value, it came 14th. In 1986, Brittany Ferries, which had bought Truckline, began a passenger service to France, and in 1989, British Channel Island Ferries came to Poole.

An increase in traffic, especially lorries going to the ferry, meant that new roads were badly needed in the east of the county. Accordingly, dual carriageways were built, to make it easy to drive in and out of the towns, and to link with the M27 and M3 motorways. Roads due north, though, remained tortuous, so that in the early 1990s a racing cyclist could travel between Bristol and Poole faster than a heavy lorry. To the west there has been some improvement, though it is little more than the building of by-passes, for example, at Bere Regis, Dorchester and Bridport. Castleman's dream of quick, easy travel to Exeter has still not come true.

In contrast with transport by road, sea and air, the railways declined. They were overworked during the war, and reduced to such a state that when peace came they had to be nationalised. Then, as road transport grew, so did the railways' losses. In 1963, the Beeching Report recommended the closure of numerous unimportant lines, many of which had never made money, even in the 19th century. Among them was the Somerset and Dorset which closed in 1966. The tangle of lines around Poole and Bournemouth was pruned until only one was left, which ran through the heart of the conurbation. For a time it looked as if there might be no railway west of Poole, but it was kept open, partly because it was needed to bring oil from Purbeck. Near empty trains, making numerous stops, continue to shuttle between Poole, Dorchester and Weymouth.

There were also important changes in the countryside. The heath, which had once been of little value, suddenly gained importance because the growth of population in east Dorset meant it was needed for building land. In 1973, for example, Lord Wimborne sold 540 acres for £7.5 million. The problem with the heath was no longer what to do with it, but how best to conserve it. Though often the despair of farmers who tried to cultivate it, the heath is far from being the dismal wilderness that Hardy portrays in *The Return of the Native*. It is radiant with colour and full of wildlife.

Agriculture revived during the Second World War, and at the end of the war the government decided the country must never again become heavily dependent on imported food, so it encouraged farmers with subsidies. Helped by these, and a general revival in the economy, farming entered a new golden age.

Huge crops of cereals were grown on the thin soils of the chalk downland, and with rotations that would have horrified the best farmers of previous centuries. One such rotation was two crops of wheat, two crops of barley and then grass, eaten off by sheep. Once, the rule had been never to take two straw crops in succession, but it became profitable to take several by using artificial fertilisers at rates of up to four hundredweight per acre. Ploughing in the grass and the sheep dung restored the organic content of the soil. Harvesting was done by combines, which even in the 1970s cost £8,000 each. Cereal growing involved heavy expenses for seed, fertilisers, sprays and machines, so it was only possible for men with capital, managing farms of anything up to 2,000 acres.

In the vale, dairying continued and farms were smaller than on the chalk. There was, though, considerable progress. After the war, the '1,000 gallon herd', that is, one with an average yield of 1,000 gallons

Truckline Ferry. (Truckline Ferries)

per cow per year, was the ideal. Before long, it was the norm, with 1,200 gallons being quite usual.

Any farm, whether on the chalk, the vale or the heath, might have a unit for the intensive rearing of livestock. A pig, when born, would weigh about $2\frac{1}{2}$ lbs, but in less than eight months it increased its size over a hundredfold, to $18\frac{1}{2}$ stone. A breeding sow would give birth to a litter every five months. Battery hens produced 20 dozen eggs each in their working lives of one year.

All farmers used machines, especially tractors. Before the war, there were 14,000 working horses in Dorset; 20 years after the war, there were hardly any. The mechanisation of the farms brought a drastic decline in the number of farm workers, which might well have meant that Dorset became a county of deserted villages, as it did after the Black Death. Instead, the villages thrived, and this was because of the motor car.

Sir Frederick Treves tells the story of a village woman of the Victorian period, who went to catch a train and remarked, 'How nice it is to see a railway station again!' But people with cars could buy homes in remote parts of Dorset without condemning themselves to isolation. Some had jobs in the towns, and commuted daily; some just wanted week-end retreats; a great many retired to the country. The more cautious lived in new houses and bungalows on neat little estates. Those with more money and, perhaps, more enterprise, renovated old properties, so that country slums that had been knocked down for £50 each in the auctions of 1919, sold for tens of thousands of pounds.

The character of the villages changed. In the first place, their condition improved. Cerne Abbas, for example, which had been in the last stages of decay, became a tourist attraction. At the same time, though, the age structure altered. Places that had once teemed with farm labourers' ragged urchins now had few children. Thirty-two village schools were closed in the county between 1957 and 1971.

Finally, there was a change that, if it is permanent, could be regarded as the most important in the history of Dorset. The Local Government Act of 1974 enlarged the boundaries of the county to include Bournemouth and Christchurch. The growth of Poole had already meant a shift in the centre of gravity, for in 1971 the town's population was 107,000, or 29% of that of the county. In 1981, Poole, Bournemouth and Christchurch had a population of 303,000, or 51% of the county's.

At the end of the 20th century, the people of Dorset could, perhaps, be forgiven for viewing their county, if not with complacency, at least with some satisfaction. In the south-east, there is a fast-growing conurbation which has enjoyed a vigorous cultural life and, for most of the time, a thriving economy. Moreover, it occupies only 6% of the county, much of the rest being unspoilt countryside, with productive, efficient farms. Most of the spectacular coastline is also largely unspoilt, in spite of the large numbers of visitors. There have been rapid, even revolutionary changes, especially in the last 50 years, and they have brought their problems, but much that is good has been preserved, and there have been worthwhile achievements.

ACKNOWLEDGEMENTS
Photographs in this book have been used with the kind permission of the following: Dorset County Museum, pages 16, 107, 157, 163, 179, 183; Dorset County Library, pages 186, 188; Poole Museums Service, page 135; The Mansell Collection, pages 154, 181; Truckline Ferries, page 203. My thanks also go to Mr Trevor Yorke for drawing the line maps, plans and diagrams.

BIBLIOGRAPHY

Adlam, Brian *The Book of Dorchester* 1981
Ashley, Harry *The Dorset Coast* 1992
Ashley, Harry *The Dorset Village Book* 1984
Bailey, A R *The Great Civil War in Dorset* 1910
Barrie, D S and Clinker, C R *The Somerset and Dorset Railway* 1978
Beamish, D and Hillier, J *The Pride of Poole 1688–1850* 1974
Beckles, G *The Bridport Story* 1953
Bessborough, Earl of, Ed. *The Diaries of Lady Charlotte Guest 1833–1852*
Body, M and West, J *Weymouth, an Illustrated History* 1983
Boswell, B *Leigh* N D ca. 1986
Bright, Mervyn *Buttony* 1971
Caird, James *English Agriculture in 1850–1851* 1852
Chadwick, Edwin *Report on the Sanitary Condition of the Labouring Population of Great Britain* 1842
Clegg, A L *A History of Dorchester* 1972
Cox, Benjamin *The Book of Blandford* 1983
Cullingford, Cecil *A History of Dorset* 1980
Cullingford, Cecil *A History of Poole* 1988
Cunliffe, Barry *Hengistbury Head* 1978
Darby, H C *Domesday England* 1964
Darby, H C & Finn, R W *Domesday Geography of South-West England* 1967
Defoe, D *Tour Through the Whole Island of Great Britain 1722–1726* 1971
Dorset County Chronicle
Dorset Natural History and Archaeological Society, Proceedings
Dorset Year Book
Dorsetshire Illustrated 1900
Dyson, T *History of Christchurch* 1954
Edwards, Elizabeth *History of Bournemouth* 1981
Fernandes, G W L and Blades A E G *Stourton Caundle* 1974
Field, N H and Bugler, *Guide to the Field Monuments of Dorset* 1973
Fowles, John *Short History of Lyme Regis* 1982
Garrett, Eric *Bradford Abbas* 1989
Gibb, J H P *The Book of Sherborne* 1981

Gibbons, A O *Cerne Abbas* 1962

Good, R *The Old Roads of Dorset* 1966

Hawkins, Desmond *Cranborne Chase* 1980

Hillier, John *Ebb Tide at Poole* 1985

Hillier, John *Victorian Poole* 1990

Hutchins, Rev. John *The History and Antiquities of Dorset* 1774

Hyams, John *Dorset* 1970

James, Jude *Wimborne Minster* 1982

Kerr, Barbara *Bound to the Soil* 1975

Lavender, R A *A Thousand Years of Christchurch* 1977

Lavington, C K *Memories of Old Blandford* 1988

Lloyd, Rachel *Dorset Elizabethans* 1967

Mackenzie, J T *Cranborne Legacy* 1987

Marlow, J *The Tolpuddle Martyrs* 1971

Medlycott, M T and Sugg, G *Sandford Orcas* 1987

Miller, Alan J *Stories from Dorset History* 1987

Miller, Alan J *Poole Turnpike Trust* 1976

Morley, Geoffrey *Smuggling in Hampshire and Dorset* 1983

Oppitz, Leslie *Dorset Railways Remembered* 1989

Padfield, George *Reflections of a Dorset Countryman* 1979

Pahl, Janice *The Rope and Net Industry of Bridport* 1959

Pevsner, N and Newman, J *Dorset (The Buildings of England Series)* 1972

Putnam, W G *Roman Dorset* 1974

Reports of Special Assistant Poor Law Commissioners on the Employment of Women and Children in Agriculture 1843

Royal Commission on Historical Monuments, Dorset 5 vols. 1952–1975

Sale, Richard *Dorset* 1985

Short, Basil *A Respectable Society, Bridport 1593–1835* 1976

Smith, H P *The History of the Borough and County of the Town of Poole* Two vols. 1948 and 1951

Stevenson, W *General View of the Agriculture of the County of Dorset* 1812

Street, Sean *Tales of Old Dorset* 1992

Sutton, Jean *The Story of Poole* 1988

Sydenham, John *The History of the Town and County of Poole* 1839

Taylor, Christopher *Dorset* 1970

Thistlethwaite, Frank *Dorset Pilgrims* 1989

Thomas, D *Regional History of Railways, Vol. 1 – The West Country* 1981

Thorn, T and C Ed. *Domesday Book: Dorset* 1983

Treves, Sir Frederick *Highways and Byways in Dorset* 1906

Victoria County History of Dorset, Vol. 2 1908

Weinstock, Maureen *Studies in Dorset History* 1953

Weinstock, Maureen *More Dorset Studies* N.D.

Wheeler, R E M *Maiden Castle, Dorset* 1972

Index

Page numbers in italics indicate illustrations